Praise for *Five Smooth Stones*

This book is a must-read. It speaks to internal issues of which many can relate in our daily lives. Prior to King David, there had been no well-known giant killers in the land of Israel. Once David killed Goliath he realized the need for giant killers and raised up many. Dr. Weatherspoon has the same assignment as David, which is, training and equipping individuals to become giant killers. Her academic training and ministerial background has shaped her understanding of the learning process. She identifies the complex giants within us (anger, guilt, lust) and gives us a strategy to defeat them.

As an N.B.A Chaplain for more than 25 years, I have watched these internal giants destroy the lives of many families. This book will help you if you are serious about character development and becoming more Christ-like. It is filled with inspirational personal testimonies that will encourage you in your battle. Thank you, Dr. Cherita Weatherspoon, for this interactive masterpiece. As an author, Board of Governors Member to Christian International with Dr. Bill Hamon, I strongly recommend this book.

Bishop Robert E. Joyce, Senior Pastor
Life Center Church
www.LifeCenterChurchMichigan.com

Riveting, thought-provoking and in-your-face accountability clearly stands out in this well-written and thought out book. I love the use of the word giants and how defeating them is portrayed with confidence and personal application throughout its pages. Although it is a compilation of authors and life experiences, its writings and themes flow seamlessly. The prayers of victory at the end of the chapters is a crescendo to each segment's final thought. This book is personal, and no subject was left in the dark place of ignorance. I also appreciated the challenge to take this body of work from enjoyable, hard-hitting and informational to a committed lifestyle. This book crosses cultural, gender, social economic and, in many cases, denominational barriers and is a must-read. Bravo, to you all.

Brenda Divers, Founder & CEO
Heart Ministry Radio
www.HeartMinistryRadio.com

In *Five Smooth Stones: Defeating the Giants Within*, Dr. Cherita Weatherspoon doesn't just identify some of the greatest giants we all face, but she lays out the plan of action that can lead you to overcome them with the strength of God himself. This book is a weapon loaded with Biblical truth. I encourage you, arm yourself with Five Smith Stones.

Katy Kazadi
Writer, Artist & Passionate Teacher of God's Word
www.KatyKazadi.com

We all face the difficult challenges of giants in our life. Dr. Cherita Weatherspoon takes an in-depth look at the internal giants and how to successfully defeat them. This extraordinary compilation of information and insight delivers the reader a systematic approach to addressing and defeating giants in your life. *Five Smooth Stones: Defeating the Giants Within* is a must read.

As you use the principles of the five smooth stones, you will find yourself defeating every giant in your life. This book is a roadmap to victory over the giants in your life!

Elder Michele D. Denson
Restoration International Worship Center
www.MDenson.com

Five Smooth Stones: Defeating the Giants Within is a user-friendly and practical handbook for everyday living. This is the kind of book that reaches across spiritual levels, from infancy through maturity. The book addresses the common Giants of ignorance, unforgiveness, worry, and negativity, which can be like pesky mosquitoes or dreadful pit bulls at various times in one's life. This book not only arms one with mosquito repellent but shows you how to tame the ferocious beast.

Marcus Ruffin, Pastor
Life Empowerment Church
www.Let-God.org

Isaiah 45:2 (KJV) says, "I will go before thee, and make the crooked places straight; I will break in pieces of the gates of brass, and cut in sunder the bars of iron."

This scripture came to mind as I was reading this book. God has leveled the playing field by giving us a guidebook on how to kick down the doors of anger, unforgiveness, ignorance, temptation and lust, low self-esteem and any other giant that tries to come against His people. These stones are our tools to slay the giant within. The prompts and exercises give us a mirror into who we are internally and what we need to sharpen to win at this thing called life.

Don't just read this as a book whose author has shared their journey but read through this book, pray and meditate and see it as a reflection of who you are, where you are and what stones you already have at your disposal to slay the giants within you.

David killed the giant with a slingshot and a stone. But he knew that he could. We too can kill the giant with what is in our hand if we believe that we can. That's what this book teaches and that is what it taught me. Believe that you can, take action, and you will.

Shelita Winfield Duke
Your Soul Impact Strategist and Christian Life Coach
www.shewinunlimited.com

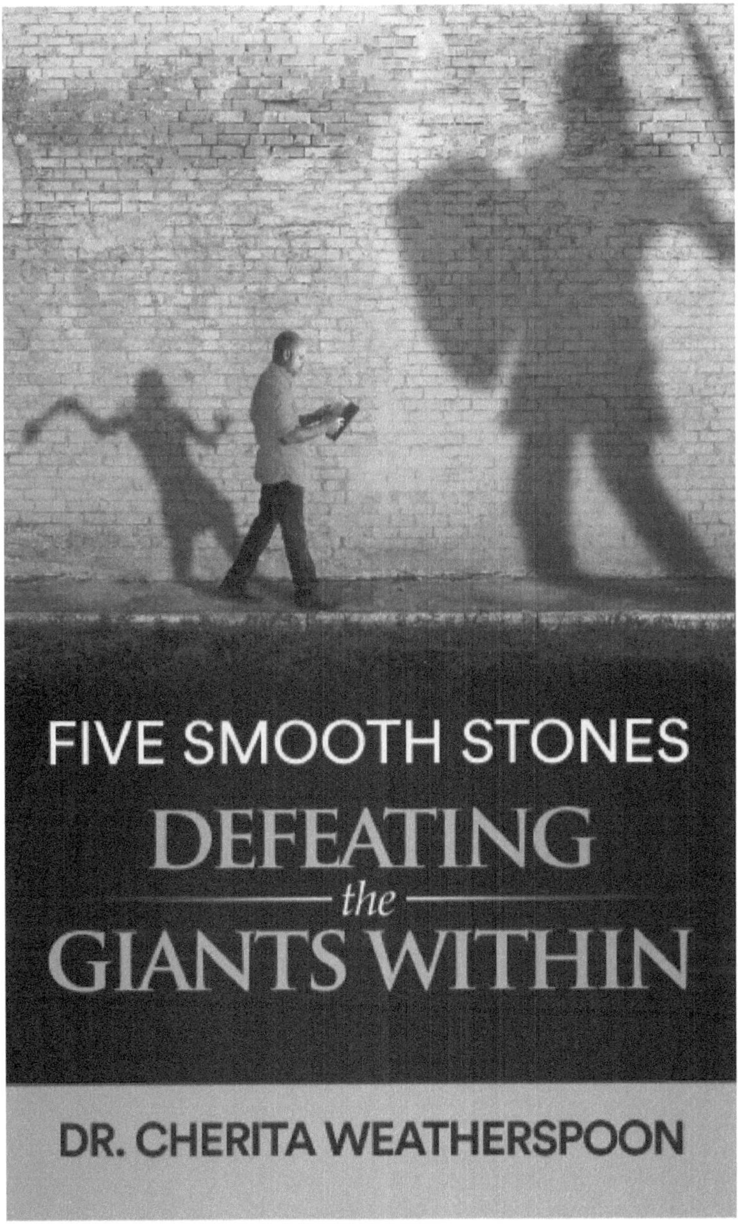

FIVE SMOOTH STONES
DEFEATING *the* GIANTS WITHIN

DR. CHERITA WEATHERSPOON

Five Smooth Stones: Defeating the Giants Within

Copyright © 2018 by Cherita G. Weatherspoon
ISBN 978-0-9983130-4-7 (ebook)
ISBN 978-0-9983130-3-0 (paperback)
ISBN 978-0-9983130-5-4 (hardcover)
Library of Congress Control Number: 2018904547

Unless otherwise noted, scripture verses are taken from the KJV of the Bible.

Scripture quotations marked NKJV are taken from the New King James Version®. Copyright © 1982 by Thomas Nelson. Used by permission. All rights reserved.

Scripture quotations marked NLT are taken from the Holy Bible, New Living Translation, copyright © 1996, 2004, 2015 by Tyndale House Foundation. Used by permission of Tyndale House Publishers, Inc., Carol Stream, Illinois 60188. All rights reserved.

Scripture quotations marked NIV are taken from THE HOLY BIBLE, NEW INTERNATIONAL VERSION®, NIV® Copyright © 1973, 1978, 1984, 2011 by Biblica, Inc.® Used by permission. All rights reserved worldwide.

Scripture quotations marked AMP are taken from the Amplified˙ Bible (AMP), Copyright © 2015 by The Lockman Foundation Used by permission. www.Lockman.org

Scripture quotations marked MSG are taken from *The Message*. Copyright © 1993, 1994, 1995, 1996, 2000, 2001, 2002. Used by permission of NavPress Publishing Group.

Greek and Hebrew translations of English words are taken from *Strong's Exhaustive Concordance: New American Standard Bible*. Updated ed. La Habra: Lockman Foundation, 1995. http://www.biblestudytools.com/concordances/strongs-exhaustive-concordance/.

Definitions, as indicated, were retrieved from:
Merriam-Webster.com. 2018. https://www.merriam-webster.com (3 July 2018)
Dictionary.com. 2018. https://dictionary.com (3 July 2018)

All rights reserved. No part of this publication may be reproduced, distributed, stored in a retrieval system, or transmitted in any form or by any means, including photocopying, recording, or other electronic or mechanical methods, without the prior written permission of the publisher, except for brief quotations in critical reviews, articles, or certain noncommercial uses permitted by copyright law.

For permission, information requests, and bulk orders write to the publisher, at: info@cheritaweatherspoon.com, Subject: Spoonfed Motivation Publications

Legal Disclaimer
This book is for informational purposes only. The author makes no claims or guarantees of outcomes or success. The content in this book should not be considered as counseling or other professional advice. Readers may implement the information included at their own discretion.

Cover Design: John Bryll L. Pulido
johnbryllpulido@gmail.com
Book Interior and E-book Design: Amit Dey

This book is dedicated to the warriors in Christ who, regardless of the difficulty of the struggle, continue to wage war for their spirit against the flesh. You are overcomers.

You Must Face the Giants to Defeat Them

Table of Contents

Foreword xiii

Acknowledgements xv

Introduction xvii

Chapter One: The Giant of Ignorance 1

Chapter Two: The Giant of Anger & Unforgiveness 23

Chapter Three: The Giant of Worry & Fear 49

Chapter Four: The Giant of Jealousy & Envy 59

Chapter Five: The Giant of Negativity 71

Chapter Six: The Giant of Guilt 81

Chapter Seven: The Giant of Pride 93

Chapter Eight: The Giant of Low Self-Esteem 105

Chapter Nine: The Giant of Temptation & Lust 121

Chapter Ten: The Giant of Control & Impatience 135

About the Authors 151

Foreword

I've always been intrigued by the story of David and Goliath outlined in I Samuel 17. When I think of Goliath, I think of a modern-day bully, someone who uses their strength or power to intimidate those who are weaker. When I read *Five Smooth Stones: Defeating the Giants Within*, it not only presented the problems that Goliath brings, but it also presented an action plan to defeat him.

Goliath can be anything that intimidates you or tries to control and destroy your life; like ignorance, anger, fear, unforgiveness, negativity, etc. All of us are dealing with something that tries to intimidate us and prevent us from stepping into our God-given purpose, thereby stopping us from fulfilling our assignment.

David strategically and purposefully placed five stones in his shepherd's bag that day - tools that he was familiar with, tools that had worked in the past. He left us an example of what we should DO when faced with similar situations.

Each one of the authors of *Five Smooth Stones* strategically and purposefully place within your hands tools that will enable you to defeat your Goliath when you do the things that have been outlined in their battle plan against the giants in your life.

If you've been bullied and taunted for too long by your personal giants, it's time for you to pick up *Five Smooth Stones* and defeat your Goliath.

Jerome Lewis, Pastor
Seeds of Greatness Ministries
www.SOGM.org

Acknowledgments

To the contributing authors who shared from their hearts and experiences to help those who read these pages, thank you for your labor and your patience. To Stacey Carter-Lane and Lois Miller, thank you for your discerning eye and red pens. To my hubby Gary and my children, Emile, Corban, Jaden and Ian, thank you for allowing me to answer the call -over and over, and over again. I pray you are inspired to pursue purpose at all costs. To my parents who always support everything that I do, thank you. To my heavenly Father, who is the giver of every perfect gift – skills, ideas and witty inventions included, thank you for giving me vision and the courage and boldness to go after it.

Introduction

Dr. Cherita Weatherspoon

> I'm not saying that I have this all together, that I have it made. But I am well on my way, reaching out for Christ, who has so wondrously reached out for me. Friends, don't get me wrong: By no means do I count myself an expert in all of this, but I've got my eye on the goal, where God is beckoning us onward—to Jesus. I'm off and running, and I'm not turning back.
>
> Philippians 3:12-14 (MSG)

This Christian walk is no leisurely stroll through life. It is a journey; perhaps we can even call it an adventure. One that takes us through bright and wide-open pastures where we lack nothing, to rugged and ragged mountain ranges that we must scale just to get a peek at what destiny awaits us. We sometimes find ourselves ducking and hiding as we make our way through the dense and dark forest, not sure of what other unwanted and gruesome surprise awaits us. Then there are times that we find ourselves relaxing, flowing in a rhythm as if we are cruising on a serene sea.

This journey will give us the opportunity to see and experience some wonderfully beautiful things, and it will also be where we experience some of our deepest hurts, our greatest failings, and face our most terrifying giants.

Giants. Yes, there will be giants. Gargantuan creatures, having an inordinate amount of strength, ferocious and menacing. We all will have to face and fight the giants that show up in our lives to block our progression forward on this journey or send us running in the opposite direction. While you may never *see* a giant in your life, believe me, they are there. They are living inside of you, waiting for the most inopportune time to express themselves or they are already in control of your life, and you either don't know it or you do, and you're ready to kill them.

These giants are no ordinary creatures. They operate in clandestine environments. While they are big, weighty, and destructive, they hide easily behind our holy facades, our demure masks, our titles, positions, and work in the church -none of which increase our righteousness. These giants are energized by our silence. They are enabled to wreak havoc in our lives when our pride does not allow us to ask for the help we need to overcome them.

Yes, we can overcome them. We can defeat the giants within. The giants that rage against our purpose and calling and mock our anointing. The giants that are holding us captive from the life that God has called us to.

I don't know about you. But I'm tired of fighting these giants. It's time to win.

If you are reading this book, you are probably tired of fighting, too. But the answer is not to give up. It is to fight with the right weapons.

> For though we walk in the flesh, we do not war according to the flesh. For the weapons of our warfare are not [a]carnal but mighty in God for pulling down strongholds, casting down arguments and every high thing that exalts itself against the knowledge of God, bringing every thought into captivity to the obedience of Christ.
>
> 2 Corinthians 10:3-5

These are spiritual giants and they can only be defeated with spiritual weapons. Your resiliency does not make you ready. Your grit is not great enough. Your will alone is not strong enough to win.

> ... God is strong, and he wants you strong. So take everything the Master has set out for you, well-made weapons of the best materials. And put them to use so you will be able to stand up to everything the Devil throws your way. This is no afternoon athletic contest that we'll walk away from and forget about in a couple of hours. This is for keeps, a life-or-death fight to the finish against the Devil and all his angels. Be prepared. You're up against far more than you can handle on your own. Take all the help you can get, every weapon God has issued, so that when it's all over but the shouting you'll still be on your feet. Truth, righteousness, peace, faith, and salvation are more than words. Learn how to apply them. You'll need them throughout your life. God's Word is an indispensable weapon. In the same way, prayer is essential in this ongoing warfare. Pray hard and long. Pray for your brothers and sisters. Keep your eyes open. Keep each other's spirits up so that no one falls behind or drops out.
>
> Ephesians 6:13-18 (MSG)

Five Smooth Stones: Defeating the Giants Within is designed to help you identify the giants in your life, embolden you to face them with courage, equip you to defeat them (once and for all), and empower you to walk worthy of the calling to which you have been called.

Each chapter, written by a different author, follows the same format:

- A personal story to demonstrate how a giant may show up in your life and to help you recognize that you are not alone in your desire and effort to defeat the giants in your life.

- Five Smooth Stones in the form of five scriptures that are expounded on by the author to help you understand what God says on the subject, how He sees you, what He desires for you, and how you can win this battle with Him.
- Encouragement for the Battle is intended to build your faith and help you understand the importance of defeating that giant.
- Make It Personal is meant to help you immediately apply what you've learned in the chapter to your life.
- A Prayer of Victory or Daily Affirmation concludes each chapter to assist you in speaking triumph, healing and wholeness into your life.

I encourage you to read this entire book - even if you don't think you are in combat with every giant identified. I promise you'll be strengthened for whatever battle you are in right now. But don't just read the book once and place it on your bookshelf. Until the battle is won, and the giant is defeated, use this book to energize and uplift you while you are on the battlefield. Read the Five Smooth Stones each day. Review and update your responses in Make It Personal. Use this book as the bag in which you carry your stones, ready to take aim at the giant whenever he advances on you.

If you want all that God has for you and desire to be fully who He created you to be, you cannot avoid this fight. It's going down. You can't run forever, and you can't stand on the sidelines talking trash forever. At some point, you will have to fight. Don't wait for the giants to bring the fight to you, take it to them, but don't go into battle ill-equipped. Get your five smooth stones and defeat the giants within.

Chapter One

THE GIANT OF IGNORANCE

Virginia (Ginny) Herndon

How readily and thoughtlessly we have embraced and appropriated in our lives the familiar idiom, *ignorance is bliss*. It has slipped off our tongue and into our hearts like Gospel truth without a moment of hesitation or consideration as to the veracity or wisdom of declaring that statement. How often have you chided, "What I don't know won't hurt me!" without a thought or evaluation of that statement's truth or impact? More than likely, you like many of us, have adopted it into your verbal arsenal and use it in your daily life without considering that it is diametrically opposed to the instruction we receive in God's Word.

Perhaps it was that previously owned sleek red sports car with a sale sign in the window that caught your eye as you drove by. It's what you have always wanted, and the price was right. Your desire to have it as your own was so strong that you decided not to check out its maintenance record or history before signing on the dotted line, rationalizing in your mind that because of its pristine outward appearance, what you didn't know couldn't be that bad. You can probably think of your own situation where you decided it was better to not know something because of fear or because what you may learn might deter you from getting what you want or make you uncomfortable or accountable; yet choosing ignorance proved detrimental in the long run. Clearly, some situations where we avoid knowledge carry profound consequences more than others.

When it comes to the Word of God, is ignorance bliss or is it disastrous? Can we be hurt by or suffer from not knowing? Is it unwise to be uninformed when it comes to truth? While we may have applied this attitude about ignorance to worldly knowledge and experienced minimal damages or undesirable consequences - when we apply it to the knowledge of God's Word we tread dangerously. Why? Because God's Word is His will for our lives and to be ignorant of His Word impacts our lives in ways that are detrimental to our destiny. Hosea 4:6 (AMP) tells us that we can be destroyed for lacking knowledge: "My people are destroyed for lack of knowledge [of My law, where I reveal My will]. Because you [the priestly nation] have rejected knowledge, I will also reject you from being My priest. Since you have forgotten the law of your God, I will also forget your children." The Message Bible translates the first portion of this verse like this: "My people are ruined because they don't know what's right or true." Isaiah 5:13 (AMP) speaks of God's people entering captivity because they have no knowledge. Proverbs 1:22 and 13:16 (AMP) clearly paints the picture of the fool as one who is without knowledge, while the prudent man is the one who deals with knowledge.

Let's define *knowledge*. The Merriam-Webster Online Dictionary uses these terms: *the fact or condition of knowing something with familiarity gained through experience or association; the range of one's information or understanding; the circumstance or condition of apprehending truth or fact through reasoning; something learned and kept in the mind.* There are various kinds of knowledge depending on what sources you read. We can agree that there is worldly knowledge that we gain from our experiences, studies, observations, relationships, and so forth. Then there is the knowledge that comes from the Lord, largely through reading and comprehending His Word of Truth and from revelation by the Holy Spirit. The latter is our focus.

So, how can we be destroyed for lack of knowledge of God's Word? It is because God's Word is our instruction manual for life.

Think of when you buy a new car or new appliance. The creators or manufacturers of those products include an operation manual because they know how those items will best serve you. If you follow the operation and maintenance directions for a new automobile and have it serviced according to the manual's instructions, you can expect to have a better running vehicle with greater longevity. The same is true for us as creations of the Creator. He too did not leave us without instructions for a victorious life. He provided our manual for living - the Holy Bible, but we are responsible for reading it and doing it if we desire to experience that victorious life. If, however, we don't read the instructions and then do them, we will most likely experience a very different outcome. Let's look at some specific examples about the importance of knowing God's Word.

In one of Paul's charges to Timothy, he says, "But as for you, continue in what you have learned and have become convinced of, because you know those from whom you learned it, and how from infancy you have known the Holy Scriptures, which are able to make you wise for salvation through faith in Christ Jesus. All Scripture is God-breathed and is useful for teaching, rebuking, correcting and training in righteousness, so that the servant of God may be thoroughly equipped for every good work" (2 Timothy 3:14-17 NIV). We search the shelves of bookstores for manuals on how to succeed at a job or project or in a relationship or circumstance. Yet in those verses we read that knowledge of God's Word, because it is breathed out by God, is valuable for teaching, reproof, correction, and training to make us complete and equipped for every good work. What a statement; what a promise! Also, we are told that these Scriptures can make us wise for salvation. While some might limit the word *salvation* only to mean the promise of eternity with the Lord, it is much more encompassing. The Greek word for salvation is *soteria*, meaning: *rescue, safety, deliver, health, salvation, save* (Strong's Concordance). So, knowledge of God's Word can make us wise through faith in all those areas. Ignorance of God's Word is ignorance of God's best for you and of the means to possess it.

God's Word provides us with so much more than a roadmap to eternity. It's also an instruction manual on how to enjoy the goodness of the Lord in the land of the living. Because of the power of God's Word, we can be equipped with an arsenal of ammunition effective in slaying every giant that opposes His plans and purpose for our lives. The giant of ignorance is at the very core of giant-slaying because knowledge of truth is the ammunition. Knowledge of His truth is the stone -the spiritual weapon that deals the deadly blow to the Goliaths in our lives. Yes, sickness is a giant. Poverty is a giant. Fear, depression, worthlessness, shame, anger, addiction are also giants - but ignorance of God's Word is the kingpin giant. We must first walk in the knowledge of truth so that we gain the understanding of how to effectively bring destruction and annihilation to every other giant.

> *God's Word provides us with so much more than a roadmap to eternity.*

That leads us to these questions: Why are we as believers, not investing the time in His Word? Why for so many, is Sunday morning the only time we crack open our Bible? Surely each one of us could present a list of legitimate reasons ranging from hectic work schedules to household responsibilities and even church and ministry work; but when we realize the high cost of low living, our excuses ring hollow. When we gain understanding of the boundless power of His Word, of the countless promises in His Word and of our delegated authority as children of God, we are robbing ourselves of great riches in every area of life, by walking in ignorance in any area of life. The truth is we cannot afford *not* to devote time with Him - reading, meditating and doing His Word. We may have been able to slide by so far, but given the times in which we live, with the increase of spiritual darkness and accelerating opposition to truth, we cannot afford to live in ignorance. We must fortify ourselves with truth which includes the assurance of our delegated authority and dominion (Luke 10:19 AMP), bolstered by unwavering faith and steadfast confidence that He holds His Word above His Name (Psalm 138:2 AMP). We must be positioned, empowered, standing at our respective posts, fully armed and educated in the Word, which is a powerful weapon. The Message Bible says in Ephesians 6:17, "God's Word is an indispensable weapon." So, just as David selected five smooth stones from the brook to hurl at Goliath (1 Samuel 17:40 NIV), the giant who was coming against him and his people; we want to be equipped with our spiritual weaponry, so we can overcome the giants that oppose us. The first giant to defeat is ignorance of His word of truth. To accomplish this, we must invest the time in His word and gain understanding and revelation of that truth - the very exercise that opposes ignorance. David had experience hurling stones out of his slingshot as he protected sheep from other animals. Therefore, when he approached Goliath he was not experimenting with unknown weapons and ammunition; he was familiar, comfortable, confident, and experienced with how to use that slingshot.

The same applies to us. If we desire to be successful in overcoming the giants that oppose us, we must become very familiar with the Sword of the Spirit (the word of God), what it says, how to use it and assured of the authority delegated to us. When we have His word on the matter and execute it, we are empowered to defeat the opposition. Remember what David said as he came against the giant, Goliath: "David said to the Philistine, 'You come against me with sword and spear and javelin, but I come against you in the name of the Lord Almighty, the God of the armies of Israel, whom you have defied. This day the Lord will deliver you into my hands, and I'll strike you down and cut off your head. This very day I will give the carcasses of the Philistine army to the birds and the wild animals, and the whole world will know that there is a God in Israel" (1 Samuel 17:45-46 NIV).

David's victory did not come because of worldly knowledge and surely not from the counsel of his elder and king - Saul, who thought he knew how David should be clothed and equipped for battling this giant. It came from his personal experience with God who had shown His faithfulness to David as he protected and tended sheep for his father. When others tried to discourage David and question his ability to defeat this Goliath who taunted the Israelites for forty days, David confidently responded, "The Lord who rescued me from the paw of the lion and the paw of the bear will rescue me from the hand of this Philistine. Saul said to David, 'Go, and the Lord be with you'" (1 Samuel 17:37 NIV).

> *If you are trying to make it on worldly knowledge alone, rest assured that will not cut it.*

David's history with God at an early age served him well as he boldly confronted this giant. We are told in 1 Samuel 17:48, 50-51 (NIV): "As the Philistine moved closer to attack him, David ran quickly toward the battle line to meet him...So David triumphed over the Philistine with a sling and a stone; without a sword in his hand he struck down the Philistine and killed him. David ran and stood over him. He took hold of the Philistine's sword and drew it from the sheath. After he killed him, he cut off his head with the sword. When the Philistines saw that their hero was dead, they turned and ran." If you are operating in ignorance of God's Word, you are taking a significant risk of missing out on the full measure of what God has provided and made available to you through the death and resurrection of His Son, Jesus Christ. If you are trying to make it on worldly knowledge alone, rest assured that will not cut it. Perhaps you have already reached that conclusion.

Just as David secured five smooth stones from the brook to defeat the giant that opposed him and his people, we can utilize God's Word as our weaponry and ammunition to defeat giants in our lives which keep us from apprehending the riches of our inheritance. If you have not appreciated the importance or necessity of knowing and doing His Word, as you read the promises and provisions He has made for you in His Word and meditate on the following scripture verses, trust that to change. May a desire to know more about what belongs to you *and* how to apprehend it be stirred up within you.

FIVE SMOOTH STONES

Stone 1

Your word is a lamp for my feet, a light on my path.

Psalm 119:105 (NIV)

We live in a dark world surrounded by many distractions and things that can cloud our hearts and minds, preventing us from clearly seeing and knowing what we should do or what path we should take. It's like waking up in the middle of the night in complete darkness and fumbling around the room trying to find the light switch. You can see, but all you see is darkness. You touch things as you move around the room trying to feel where you are. You determine your position in the room by what you feel rather than what you know. You hope you find the light switch before you stump your toe. Too late! Ouch!

Many of us are fumbling and stumbling through life just like this. In the dark. We're making decisions about where to go and what to do based on our feelings, hoping we don't get hurt in the process. But God has given us the master plan. One that is *son*-powered and can be read in the darkest of places. As you read it, the light becomes brighter and your path becomes clearer. You're no longer limited to making decisions based on your feelings. You can make decisions based on the understanding and wisdom gained through learning what God says about you, what He desires for you, and how He wants you to operate in this world.

When we use God's word to light our path, we gain wisdom and we develop the ability to discern the spirits at work within situations and the hearts of people we interact with. We are empowered to make Godly decisions and we gain the creative ability to solve problems.

Stone 2

This Book of the Law shall not depart from your mouth, but you shall read [and meditate on] it day and night, so that you may be careful to do [everything] in accordance with all that is written in it; for then you will make your way prosperous, and then you will be successful.

Joshua 1:8 (AMP)

God's word will not only lead us out of the dark places of this world, but it will lead us into a place that is peaceful, full of His light, and where His desires for us are made manifest. This verse tells us that following God's instructions leads us to prosperity and success. More specifically, it speaks to how our consistency in speaking, reading and studying God's word enables us to follow His word, which makes our path (the path that His word has lighted for us) beneficial and it will ultimately lead to our success – living the life that God planned for each us.

Stone 3

In whom are hidden all the treasures of wisdom and knowledge [regarding the word and purposes of God].

Colossians 2:2-3 (AMP)

Everything you need to know, from a spiritual perspective, to make your way through this world, is in the word of God. Wisdom to handle any situation you face can be found between Genesis and Revelations. There is nothing new under the sun. For any situation you are facing in your life, wisdom can be found in God's word. Your issue may look new, but the root issue underneath is nothing new in this world or to God.

Stone 4

And do not be conformed to this world [any longer with its superficial values and customs], but be transformed and progressively changed [as you mature spiritually] by the renewing of your mind [focusing on godly values and ethical attitudes], so that you may prove [for yourselves] what the will of God is, that which is good and acceptable and perfect [in His plan and purpose for you].

Romans 12:2 (AMP)

There is the world's way, and there is God's way. They lead in opposite directions, never to converge. Whichever path you choose to take you are making the decision to change into something other than who you are. If you choose to follow the world's path you are choosing to conform - to imitate and adapt to the world's way of being and doing. The word *conform* can also be defined as *rebel*. So, when you conform to the world, you are rebelling against who God created you to be.

If you choose to follow God's path, you are choosing to transform – convert or renovate who you are now to become all of who God desires you to be. Both changes come about through what you set your mind on. What you think about. What you choose to believe. What you focus on. All these things will eventually show up in your life. When you focus on the things of the world, you become increasingly worldly in your words and actions. The world's values become your values. The world's way of doing things becomes your way of doing things.

When you focus on the things of God, you become more like God and more in tune with God's will for your life. God's values become your values. His thoughts become your thoughts. His ways become your ways.

You are going to grow in the knowledge of something. You have the power to choose whether that knowledge is developed in the world's system or in God's system. Whichever system you are more knowledgeable in is the one that will direct how you live your life.

Stone 5

For His divine power has bestowed on us [absolutely] everything necessary for [a dynamic spiritual] life and godliness, through true and personal knowledge of Him who called us by His own glory and excellence.

2 Peter 1:3 (AMP)

Your power, your wisdom and your discernment increase as you grow in the knowledge of God. Your knowledge of God grows by reading His word and hearing His voice. You can only hear (discern) His voice by becoming familiar with how He talks. The best way to learn how He talks is to read His word. It all and always comes back to God's word. Everything we need to live this life and to operate in this world can be learned through His word. There is no need to be ignorant; however, you can choose to be willfully ignorant. But, remember, that ignorance is no defense for not following God's word when His word is accessible to you.

ENCOURAGEMENT FOR THE BATTLE

Ignorance of God's Word is not bliss. Dr. Kenneth E. Hagin has been attributed with saying, "Faith begins where the will of God is known." If we are ignorant of God's Word, we are ignorant of His will and do not have the foundation on which to operate in faith. One definition of *will* is *divine determination*. Just as we have attorneys draw wills for us regarding how we want our estates disposed and what we want to occur after our death, God has provided us His Word, which is His will. A will does not become effective until death occurs. God's will is effective now. Because of Jesus' death and resurrection, we presently have access to that which He has provided. We are the beneficiaries named in His will and have access to our inheritance now. We, however, must know what He has provided and how to access and apprehend it. Without the knowledge contained within His Word, we remain ignorant and fail to take hold of that which rightfully belongs to us.

If we do not know, for example, what God's will is concerning healing, how can we operate in faith, believing for health and wholeness? Lack of knowledge of His Word implies ignorance of His will. How many of you have prayed, "Lord, if it be your will, heal me of this disease," or "Lord, if it be your will, provide me with the means to support my family." Those are prayers that illustrate ignorance of God's Word. God, in His atonement, has provided for our health, peace, and provision through Jesus: "Beloved, I pray that in every way you may succeed and prosper and be in good

> *If we do not know, for example, what God's will is concerning healing, how can we operate in faith, believing for health and wholeness?*

health [physically], just as [I know] your soul prospers [spiritually]" (3 John 1:2 AMP). "Let them shout for joy and rejoice, who favor my vindication and want what is right for me; Let them say continually, 'Let the Lord be magnified, who delights and takes pleasure in the prosperity of His servant'" (Psalm 35:27 AMP). "You will keep in perfect and constant peace the one whose mind is steadfast [that is, committed and focused on You - in both inclination and character], Because he trusts and takes refuge in You [with hope and confident expectation]" (Isaiah 26:3 AMP).

This is His will and we learn it by reading His Word. Without this knowledge how can we expect to attain the abundant life that Jesus described in John 10:10 (AMP)? God's Word makes it clear in Psalm 91:16 (AMP) that He desires us to walk in health and be satisfied with long life. This is a very important truth that we may not know if we are ignorant of His Word. Isaiah 53:4-5 (AMP) says, "But [in fact] He has borne our griefs, And He has carried our sorrows and pains; Yet we [ignorantly] assumed that He was stricken, struck down by God and degraded and humiliated [by Him]. But He was wounded for our transgressions, He was crushed for our wickedness [our sin, our injustice, our wrongdoing]; The punishment [required] for our well-being fell on Him, And by His stripes (wounds) we are healed." How senseless for us to not take hold of our blood-bought inheritance as His children!

God's will is for us to know His Word. By having intimate knowledge of His Word, we know Him, His will for our lives, His precious promises and how they are fulfilled. He says, "Call to Me and I will answer you, and tell you [and even show you] great and mighty things, [things which have been confined and hidden], which you do not know and understand and cannot distinguish" (Jeremiah 33:3 AMP). We read in 1 Timothy 2:4 (AMP) that the Lord desires our salvation so that we can know and understand his divine truth. His will is for us to walk in understanding of His Truth, of what He has to say to us. His will is for us to walk in freedom and deliverance (John 8:32 AMP, 2 Peter 1:3 AMP). Because He is the Word (John1:1 NIV), as we grow in the knowledge of His word our lives should reflect the truth of 2 Peter 1:3: "For His divine power has bestowed on us [absolutely] everything necessary for [a dynamic spiritual] life and godliness, through true and personal knowledge of Him who called us by His own glory and excellence." However, we first must know what rightfully belongs to us as His heirs.

* * *

Have you ever seen in a newspaper, a list of individuals who have unclaimed property? I recall a couple of years ago while vacationing, I was reading the newspaper and there were multiple pages with numerous columns of names and corresponding unclaimed property. Those individuals had money or real estate that rightfully belonged to them, yet they did not have access to it because they did not know they were entitled to it. Immediately I thought of the children of God; you and me, who have great and limitless deposits in our accounts, provision made by Jesus Christ through His death and resurrection. Yet many of us never possess those resources that have been earmarked with our names and set aside for us, because of ignorance.

A few years ago, my mother received a letter in the mail notifying her of some unclaimed property and monies which rightfully belonged to her. However, because she did not know about the money prior to receiving the letter, she did not have it in her possession. Even when she was made aware of it, the check was not included with the letter. The letter instructed what she needed to do to secure the funds belonging to her. She followed the process and completed the required forms; however, she did not immediately receive the check. About two months later, she received the full sum of money due; ultimately possessing what belonged to her. Had she not known, she would not be in possession of what rightfully belonged to her. While it wasn't a life-changing amount of money, it was still rightfully hers. But without that knowledge, she couldn't claim it. Do you want what is rightfully yours? If so, open God's word to find out what He has for you.

Ignorance of God's Word translates to ignorance of God's will. Ignorance of God's will for our lives translates to living a life unfulfilled, despite the provision God made for each of His children through His Son, Jesus Christ. Ignorance is bliss? Hardly! When it comes to God's Word, it is imperative that we know it for the sake of our lives. We are exhorted in Ephesians 5:17 (AMP), "Therefore do not be foolish and thoughtless, but understand and firmly grasp what the will of the Lord is." God's will is that you have knowledge of Him and His Word; He makes this clear to us throughout the Old and New Testaments. He repeatedly tells us to grow in the knowledge of Him, and He confirms His desire and willingness to teach us.

God did His part by helping us to walk in understanding. He not only provided us with His will in His Word but also sent the Holy Spirit as our Teacher to open the eyes of our understanding so that we can comprehend His Word and apply it in our lives. As my Pastor, Jerome Lewis, says; "The Holy Spirit is our unlimited supply of divine revelation." God has already done His part. Our responsibility is reading, believing and *doing* His Word with the help of the Holy Spirit who brings revelation.

In the Christian faith, the word *sovereignty* is an abused term. It has given the believer license to be lazy and place all responsibility on God. When things do not go as desired or promised in His Word, because God is sovereign, He gets blamed for what did not work. Just because He is sovereign, we cannot expect God's will for our lives to magically unfold without any participation on our part. For example, when people die prematurely, often you hear conclusions that "it must have been God's will because if He wanted him to live, he would be alive." Jesse Duplantis, in the *Sovereignty of God*, says it like this: "The truth is that God is sovereign in that He can do what He wants, and when He wants but He has made a choice to bind Himself by His own Word." Duplantis adds that when things don't happen as we expect or desire, our reasoning about His sovereignty "lets everybody off the hook - except God." He gets "accused of killing somebody, for withholding the healing Blood of Jesus and for going back on His Word. This is wrong." God tells us, "I will not violate my covenant or alter what my lips have uttered" (Psalm 89:34 NIV). While the Lord God is sovereign, He has given us free will. The question is do we exercise our free will to invest time in His Word so that we know Him, know what belongs to us as His children and learn how to appropriate it with our faith and the words of our mouth that have creative power. After all, "Death and life are in the power of the tongue, And those who love it and indulge it will eat its fruit and bear the consequences of their words" (Proverbs 18:21 AMP) and, "For by your words you will be acquitted, and by your words you will be condemned" (Matthew 12:37 NIV).

> *The promise of prosperity and success in all areas of life is tied to knowing, believing and doing His Word.*

Growing in the knowledge of His Word is our responsibility and for our benefit. In 2 Timothy 2:15 (AMP) we are instructed to: "Study and do your best to present yourself to God approved, a workman [tested by trial] who has no reason to be ashamed, accurately handling and skillfully teaching the word of truth." In 1 Timothy 2:4 (AMP), the Lord speaks of His desire for "… all people to be saved and to come to the knowledge and recognition of the [divine] truth." All His promises are contained in His Word, according to 2 Corinthians 1:20 (AMP). However, if we are ignorant of His Word and ignorant of His promises, how can we expect to see those promises realized in our lives? Joshua 1:8 (AMP) proclaims, "This Book of the Law shall not depart from your mouth, but you shall read [and meditate on] it day and night, so that you may be careful to do [everything] in accordance with all that is written in it; for then you will make your way prosperous, and then you will be successful." The promise of prosperity and success in all areas of life is tied to knowing, believing and doing His Word. We, however, cannot accomplish that with a periodic or casual glance at His Word; instead, we should be purposefully attentive to His Word always.

* * *

Merriam-Webster defines *meditate* as follows: *to engage in contemplation or reflection; to engage in mental exercise for the purpose of reaching a heightened level of spiritual awareness; to focus one's thoughts on; to reflect on or ponder over; to plan or project in the mind.* A single, periodic glance at the Word will not change our lives; but meditating on it, having an intimate knowledge of it, allowing it to go around and around in our mind, over and over, will produce change.

Ignorance of God's word is a giant we want to defeat. No shortcut exists to defeating this giant apart from being faithful and consistent hearers, readers, believers and doers of His Word. We slay the giant of ignorance by knowing, believing and appropriating Truth. What does God's Word say about our ability as believers to understand His Word? 1 Corinthians 2:14-16 (AMP) says, "But the natural [unbelieving] man does not accept the things [the teachings and revelations] of the Spirit of God, for they are foolishness [absurd and illogical] to him; and he is incapable of understanding them, because they are spiritually discerned and appreciated, [and he is unqualified to judge spiritual matters]. But the spiritual man [the spiritually mature Christian] judges all things [questions, examines and applies what the Holy Spirit reveals], yet is himself judged by no one [the unbeliever cannot judge and understand the believer's spiritual nature]. For who has known the mind and purposes of the Lord, so as to instruct Him? But we have the mind of Christ [to be guided by His thoughts and purposes]."

As a believer in Christ Jesus, you have 24/7 access to the Holy Spirit whose many roles include teacher. As you open pages of the Holy Scriptures, ask the Holy Spirit to bring illumination, and He is only too eager to oblige. See what a difference it makes in your understanding as you invite the Holy Spirit to open the eyes of your understanding and bring supernatural revelation of Truth. We have not because we ask not (James 4:2 NIV) and that applies to knowing and understanding God's Word. You have the mind of Christ. You can understand His Word, but you must open the Bible, meditate on it and do what it says.

There is no short-cut to becoming knowledgeable of His Word. Like anything else, you can make this pursuit of knowledge a religious activity - all form and no substance. How many times have you opened the Bible to get your obligatory morning or evening devotions out of the way, as if you are doing God a favor? I have. In fact, I can recall doing just that one day and then heard the Lord say, "Don't do this for My benefit." Even as I pen the words of this devotion focusing on the importance of knowing God's Word - I realize some who read this will engage in another religious callisthenic, packing this into an overloaded day out of obligation. Undoubtedly, when you invest time in God's Word, you will reap blessings. He tells us that the entrance of His Word gives light (Psalm 119:130 AMP) and through His precepts we get understanding (Psalm 119:104 AMP). Grace and peace are multiplied through the knowledge of God and of Jesus (2 Peter 1:2 AMP). Nevertheless, we want to approach our time in His Word with the right frame of mind, with the right heart motive - not as an obligatory exercise, but as a privilege and an opportunity to come face to face with the Living God who is the Word.

We want to understand and realize that reading the Word is a divine encounter with Truth, coming into His presence where there is fullness of joy. So, what is your mindset as you commit to regular and faithful studying of God's Word as part of your daily life? If you are at the place where it is a religious experience, may it become a coveted encounter. If it has been a discipline, may it become a desire, for it is as vital to you as food and water to your natural body. When you open His Word to study, you are not reading words on a page, but meeting a Person. You will become the blessed beneficiary of the bountiful harvest that results not from walking in ignorance, but in the understanding and execution of His marvelous Word which is His will and sustenance for your life.

> *Fall in love with the one who is the Word and whose desire is for you to know Him intimately.*

So, as you purpose to defeat the giant of ignorance of His Truth in your life, do so out of a relationship with the one who is the lover of your soul and not out of a religious obligation. Fall in love with the one who is the Word and whose desire is for you to know Him intimately. It's God's love letter to you. Feast on His truth. Invite the Holy Spirit to bring illumination. Meditate on it to extract the sweet, life-giving honey of that word. Advance continually in your pursuit of truth and witness the glorious harvest that will ensue.

Ignorance is not bliss but foolish. The knowledge of His Word of Truth enables you to know Him intimately and to apprehend the boundless riches of your royal inheritance as a child of the Most High God. Walk in knowledge, not ignorance!

MAKE IT PERSONAL

1. Have you ever confessed that you do not spend much time in God's Word because it is too difficult to understand? Well, if you have received Jesus as your Lord and Savior, the Holy Spirit has taken up residence in you and He is your personal tutor; on call, day and night. How does knowing and believing this, change your belief that you cannot understand God's Word?

   _____
   _____
   _____

_____

_____

_____

2. Do you need to break agreement with the lie you confessed that you cannot understand God's Word? It's easy to do. Simply repent of wrong believing and replace that lie with Truth. Confess it aloud as often as you need until you believe it. Say something like, *Father, forgive me for believing the lie that I cannot understand the Word of God because it is too difficult. I repent of that lie and break agreement with it. Instead, I confess that I have the mind of Christ and can do all things through You, with Whom all things are possible. Thank You that I have the Holy Spirit as my Teacher and as I ask He will guide me in all Truth, grant me understanding and bring illumination so that I can and will comprehend this Word that You have made available to me and want me to know, understand, believe and do. In Jesus' Name.*

When you open God's Word, you come face to face with Jesus. You are not just reading words on a page; you are encountering the Living God. Open your Bible to John 1:1 and record that verse below: _____

_____

_____

3. According to that verse, who is The Word? _____

_____

_____

4. In the space provided below, jot down your plan of attack for becoming more faithful in spending time daily in God's Word.

_____

_____

_____

_____

_____

_____

5. As you read through the Word, make a list of verses beyond those found in this devotion, that speak about the knowledge of God, the benefits we reap from it, God's will for us concerning it, and anything else that builds the case for being knowers, believers, and doers of His Word.

    Book/Chapter/Verse: _____

    _____

    _____

    Book/Chapter/Verse: _____

    _____

    _____

    Book/Chapter/Verse: _____

    _____

    _____

    Book/Chapter/Verse: _____

    _____

6. Don't allow the study of God's word to become an obligatory exercise. Think about when you meet a dear friend for coffee or sit across the table from someone with whom you love spending time. That's how it should be when you sit down with Jesus. After all, He is the word. He longs for your presence, for you to increasingly know Him. He paid the ultimate price to provide everything for you and what a blessing for Him to see you partake in the blessings He secured through

the brutal whipping, bloodshed, ridicule, untold suffering and inhumane death on the cross. Praise God He is risen, and He is seated at the right hand of God and you are seated with Him. Read Ephesians 2:6 and write it below:

_____

_____

_____

PRAYER OF VICTORY

Gracious and loving Father, thank you for your word which is sharper than any two-edged sword. Thank you that your word makes clear the way of eternal salvation and contains all the instruction necessary to experience a triumphant life here on earth. Thank you that your word will not return void, but it will accomplish that which you have purposed it to do as I believe it and act on it. Thank you, that as I wield your word from the slingshot of my mouth that I will defeat the giants in my life as successfully as David overcame Goliath with the words he spoke. Thank you that as I speak in agreement with your word that your angels hearken to do your bidding. I purpose to do my part. I refuse ignorance of your word but instead choose to pursue and walk in knowledge and understanding of your truth. Thank you for the Holy Spirit who is my teacher. Thank you that I have the mind of Christ and am fully able to comprehend your word. I am confident that the more time I spend with you in your word, the more I will receive revelation that will come from that time together. Because your word is your will, as I grow in my understanding of it and speak it in faith out of my mouth, I will realize countless blessings and enjoy the inheritance that your Son Jesus, died to give me. In Jesus' Name. Amen.

Chapter Two

THE GIANT OF ANGER & UNFORGIVENESS

Gregory Nicholson

I grew up in Philadelphia the youngest of four (two sisters, one brother). Both of my parents worked and raised us in a very strong Christian household. My parents were involved in various roles and ministries in the church and they made sure we were active participants as well. We went to church every Sunday, which usually included both a morning and afternoon service. We also attended multiple bible conventions and meetings throughout the year. In a nutshell, we were always in or going to something related to church. We were Pentecostal; God was at the center of our lives and being in church was what we did.

We were taught at home and at church to look holy, talk holy and act holy. There was a lot of emphasis placed on spiritual appearances. Everyone around us determined your Christian commitment by what they saw. If you looked a certain way, you couldn't be saved. In some ways, it makes sense. The Bible says in John 13:35 (AMP), "By this everyone will know that you are My disciples, if you have love and unselfish concern for one another." James 1:22 (NIV) talks about doing the word and not simply hearing the word, so looking and acting holy is kind of part of it. The problem is that acting holy towards one another does not mean you have love for one another. It just means that on the outside, you act like all is well. There is no guarantee that you have a true commitment to love in your heart; which is where God and Godly love reside.

Why is this important? It's all about the effect it had on me. All this focus on acting holy meant when something bothered you or you had an issue with something, you didn't really address it; especially things that were very important to you and meant a great deal. We would just store those things in our little closet and they would just pile up. This was the culture in my home, where confrontation or the concern of confrontation was bigger than anything else. We felt we were fulfilling the being holy mantra because we looked holy and forgiving; didn't start arguments, fights or confront people. We were more holy because we acted as if everything was ok. The reality was that on the inside, at any given time - we could be bitter, resentful and feel things while our anger closet was filling up. As a result, I developed a masked or avoidance style of anger, which caused me to store and list everything you said and did that bothered me. While trying to suppress and hide my feelings, I was just growing angrier. This pent-up anger made it easy not to forgive people. I mean come on, I have a whole closet full of things you've said and done.

Overall, we did not have serious issues within my family. We didn't have a lot of drama because I had good parents, but the giants were being formed. Satan was twisting what we thought were good Christian behaviors in a way which caused me to miss out on understanding true Godly love and forgiveness towards others. It isn't about showing love, but about having love first. Having love on the inside is where it starts. The Bible talks quite often about being deeply rooted in love, and when you have these roots, your actions towards others are more genuine about loving and forgiving, no matter what.

Eventually, I got married, and my wife is the one who experienced the effects of this masked anger and unforgiving giant. She grew up in a household full of confrontation. In some ways, it was very refreshing, but it could be unfiltered at times. This caused me (in my masked anger approach), to fill my closet with various remarks, comments, and responses that I just did not like. Rather than work those things out lovingly, I stored them. Then one day, something is said or done and my closet door swings open and it all comes out. Or I might do things I know she doesn't like due to my anger or being unable to forgive. It could be as simple as limiting our discussion or responses over several days or barely talking at all. I justified it because I did not retaliate in an angry way (at least outwardly). I was the better person because I watched what I said to people. It didn't matter that I knew it bothered her. Maybe next time she won't say what she said. This was my mantra; I looked holy, acted holy, and I talked holy most of the time. I was not causing any issues, so I was in the right (at least that was how I felt). This was another example of Satan using his giant of anger to lead to unforgiveness, which led me to do other things to cause trouble in our relationship.

> *God's greatest act towards man was Him restoring our relationship back to Him.*

I did not really understand the stones I was being armed with concerning love and forgiveness, but they were right in front of me the entire time. The Bible says in John 3:16 (NIV), "For God so loved the world that he gave his one and only Son, that whoever believes in him shall not perish but have eternal life." God's greatest act towards man was Him restoring our relationship back to Him. This act was based on His love for us and His desire to forgive us of our wrong doings no matter what. He could have kept a list and judged us accordingly; instead, even in our wrongdoing - He chose love and forgiveness. Romans 5:8 (AMP) says, "But God clearly shows and proves His own love for us, by the fact that while we were still sinners, Christ died for us." What an awesome God we serve!

Until I really began to understand love, I did not see the benefit of avoiding unforgiveness and the issues tied to unresolved anger.

1 Corinthians 13:4-8 (NIV) says, "Love is patient, love is kind. It does not envy, it does not boast, it is not proud. It does not dishonor others, it is not self-seeking, it is not easily angered, it keeps no record of wrongs. Love does not delight in evil but rejoices with the truth. It always protects, always trusts, always hopes, always perseveres. Love never fails..." When you see how the Bible describes the actions of love, you begin to see how much we need to do to completely commit to having love for one another; because when you do, you can't fail because love does not fail.

It is those three words, "love never fails" and knowing that Jesus came to destroy the works of the devil (1 John 3:8 NIV), which lays the foundation of knowing the giants Satan created cannot win. Satan only wins if we allow him to win. The smooth stones, the Word that God gave us, wins. God is love and the ultimate creator of forgiveness - which is at the core of this imminent defeat. Even if you are battling these giants today, you will win if you choose to follow God's ways. Just like David, we must know who we are and be willing to throw the stones of love and forgiveness. We should not do what God says to do about anger and forgiving because of the consequences, but because of an understanding of the pitfalls the anger and unforgiving giants represent. This should help us understand why we should not let those giants have their way. In the end, the choice will be yours.

In today's world, the giants of anger and unforgiveness are all around us. One of the reasons anger is so common is because it is part of our God-given DNA. We were made in His image. Just like He can be angry, so can we. The difference is in how we process anger versus how God does. God only experiences anger; He uses it out of His love for us and the need to address situations like sin. After He handles the situation, anger is no longer needed. The Israelites in the wilderness have plenty of examples of God being angry with Moses or people. They murmured, revolted against Moses, built the golden calf, etc. (see Exodus). Though they experienced his anger, it was just a moment; then he would continue to operate towards them out of love. We become angry, and because we process it differently, it leads to wrongdoing, unforgiveness and other acts that God does not want us to do to one another. God is very clear on what anger can lead to and gives several warnings in His Word. Unforgiveness is also a giant He clearly addresses as well. He is the God of forgiveness, and His expectation is for us to be totally forgiving of our fellow man through His examples towards us. How we process anger and fail to forgive are closely related; one usually comes with the other. Until we fully understand that love is the key to processing anger so that it does not lead to unforgiveness, this giant will continue to taunt us. Below are scriptures that will hopefully help you begin to understand God's stance with these two giants and the issues associated with them.

Proverbs 29:22 (NIV) hits the spot immediately regarding what the anger giant can do: "An angry person stirs up conflict, and a hot-tempered person commits many sins." The definition of strife is a bitter and sometimes violent conflict or struggle (Merriam-Webster.com). The warning couldn't be any more direct. When you are angry - at some point, you will cause strife. Strife is on the list of what the bible refers to as *the* "acts of the flesh" in Galatians 5:19-21 (NIV). The acts of the flesh solidify the fact that this giant is of the devil and he wants us to be led and ruled by it. This anger starts on the inside and manifests as strife. As the giant gets bigger (you become furious), it leads to transgression. *Transgression* is defined as a *violation of a law or command; and sin* (Dictionary.com). This is a clear warning that giving place to this giant will cause you to progress into territory that is out of bounds – out of the bounds of God's love. The key is not to let it get a hold of us in the first place. Satan is trying to use his giants to get a foothold. It is the foothold that gives him access. Once he has access, the manifestations of his access are experienced.

The bible says in Ephesians 4:26-27 (NIV), "'In your anger do not sin': Do not let the sun go down while you are still angry, and do not give the devil a foothold." Anger is like a kettle on a stove. If left on the fire, it will bubble over. Anger left to steep overnight is truly a sleeping giant which will awaken ready to fight. There were many nights in the past when I went to bed angry, and when I awakened, I basically started where I left off. What did it lead to? Malice, bitterness, unforgiveness, etc. These are all the things that come from the foothold Satan establishes. In the worst case, strife leads to a transgression which may be a regret that can't be fixed, like murder, infidelity, or a physical attack. It may seem far-fetched, but there are many people in prison today who killed out of passion; this is a clear example of the transgression anger can lead to when you let this giant direct you.

> ***It is the filling of His Word that causes us to respond positively instead of being provoked.***

Everything in the natural starts in the spiritual realm. The spiritual realm, in this case, is your heart or your spirit. Ecclesiastes 7:9 (AMP), clearly shows how you can be led by your spirit man or the Holy Spirit; you have a choice: "Do not be eager in your heart to be angry, For anger dwells in the heart of fools." Something happens, and you say to yourself, "I will not let my spirit be provoked." The question then becomes, who is at the source of this provocation. It is the devil who is trying to get you to give in to anger, which leads to strife and transgression. The Bible says in Ephesians 6:12 (NIV), "For our struggle is not against flesh and blood, but against the rulers, against the authorities, against the powers of this dark world and against the spiritual forces of evil in the heavenly realms." The battle that is occurring is where the provocation comes from. We must let God fight our battles and let His Word fill us and tell us what to do. It is the filling of His Word that causes us to respond positively instead of being provoked. Luke 6:45 (NIV) says, "A good man brings good things out of the good stored up in his heart, and an evil man brings evil things out of the evil stored up in his heart. For the mouth speaks what the heart is full of." The anger giant wants us to be provoked but God's word in us trumps it. So, what is the flip side of all of this? You can allow anger to live with you and you can be led by it. How did Ecclesiastes 7:9 (AMP) say it? "Anger dwells in the heart of fools." You see, fools are people who act unwisely. They are deficient in judgment, sense or understanding. In other words, fools don't make good decisions. Fools allow their spirits to be led by anger. We are not fools because we are aware of the schemes and wiles of the devil. There shouldn't be any situation in life where you want to be defined by what a fool does.

I mentioned earlier that God sent His only begotten son for the forgiveness of our sins. He did it out of His love for us, which is the basis for His desire to forgive. We did not earn salvation. The bible says it is a gift (see Romans 6:23 and Ephesians 2:8-9 NIV). These verses begin to lay the foundation for why the gift that God gave us should be freely given by us. The giant of unforgiveness is so big that God is not willing to forgive us if we don't forgive others (see Matthew 6:15 NIV). If He can't forgive us of our sins, then we can't get access to the gift of forgiveness He has for us. Unforgiveness is a sin because He commands us to forgive and clearly states the consequences of not obeying Him. Think about it; with all the sinning we commit, imagine how easy it is to be in a sinful state. We are born into sin; we have a sinful nature. What we think, say and do can all be sins. We need to be forgiven, and if we aren't, we are exposing ourselves to be separated from God. This is a very strong position for God to take, but it shows how important forgiveness is to Him. I know so many people who are angry with family members and friends with whom they have no intention of forgiving for something they did years ago. In some instances, the offenses were committed so long ago they don't even remember the details. Even if they did, is it worth going against God and being separated from Him? Look at it this way, Ephesians 5:1 (AMP) says, "Therefore become imitators of God [copy Him and follow His example], as well-beloved children [imitate their father]." It's as simple as that… just do it. Psalm 37:8 (AMP) warns us against anger and touches on how it can lead to wrath; reiterating that anger leads to things we should not do. "Cease from anger and abandon wrath; Do not fret; it leads only to evil." Wrath is forceful or vindictive anger. Vindictiveness and vengeful anger is all about getting even because you are bitter, upset and have not forgiven someone for what happened. The bible says in Romans 12:19 (NIV), "Do not take revenge, my dear friends, but leave room for God's wrath, for it is written: It is mine to avenge; I will repay, says the Lord." This tells us that it is not our responsibility to get back at people. God ensures that everyone reaps the harvest from what they have sown. When we let God handle these situations, we prevent ourselves from reaping our own harvest of unforgiveness. James 1:20 (NIV) says, "…because human anger does not produce the righteousness that God desires." In other words, when we use or experience wrath, the outcomes are not good. We will end up doing something wrong or evil. Remember, the devil is doing all he can to get you to make wrong decisions. When acting in anger, you won't produce what God wants you to, and you take yourself out of the grace of God.

Matthew 18:35 (NIV) reminds me of my previous statements where I mentioned the importance of showing love from your heart versus a hollow act; "This is how my heavenly Father will treat each of you unless you forgive your brother or sister from your heart." Not only are acts of showing love hollow; they are not sustainable. This is why your outside can show one thing, but your heart (or spirit) has other intentions. This scripture is how Jesus ends a parable about an unmerciful servant. The servant who is forgiven of his debts chooses not to forgive his servant in the same manner. The servant is punished, and Jesus uses this to define further how we will be dealt with if we don't forgive. Again, the key here is true

> *If we keep iniquities in our heart, we are negatively impacting our prayer life.*

forgiveness defined by the heart. Just as you accept Christ from your heart, you must do the same with forgiveness. No little closets where you accept apologies - but plan to get vengeance later or end up using what happened against someone later. Psalm 66:18 (AMP) discusses issues of the heart; it says, "If I regard sin and baseness in my heart [that is, if I know it is there and do nothing about it], The Lord will not hear [me]." There are two points to take from this. First, if you choose to keep iniquity in your heart, there are consequences. Second, sin separates you from God and iniquity establishes a wall between you and God that prevents Him from hearing your prayers. As Christians, speaking to God is critical in our relationship with our Heavenly Father. None of us can be successful in this world without being able to talk to Him. If we keep iniquities in our heart, we are negatively impacting our prayer life. Satan wants us to be as far from God as possible. If he can use specific giants to cause separation because of sin and the consequence results in prayers not being heard; that is perfect for him. That means we won't meet our full potential. He wants whatever he can get because the devil came to kill, steal and destroy (John 10:10). He will take whatever he can get, any way he can get it.

In the end, the giants of anger and unforgiveness, are just a few of the weapons the devil uses. As big as these giants may appear, they are not bigger than love and forgiveness. What we must remember is: 1) Jesus came to defeat the weapons of the devil (see 1 John 3:8 NIV) which means we win; 2) We know love never fails; and, 3) We have a choice to follow God and His Holy Spirit, or we can give in to the flesh and follow it. It is up to us if we choose to process anger through love and forgive one another or allow anger to lead us to unforgiveness and all the strife and transgressions it will cause. God's desire (and mine too), is for us to make the right choice. Deuteronomy 30:19 (NIV) says, "This day I call the heavens and the earth as witnesses against you that I have set before you life and death, blessings and curses. Now choose life, so that you and your children may live."

God wants us to choose life and if we do, according to this verse - we will live, and our children will live as well. In John 10:10 (AMP), God promises us an abundant life. It is accessible to us when we walk in the same love and forgiveness that Jesus walked in.

FIVE SMOOTH STONES

Stone 1

The second is like it, 'You shall love your neighbor as yourself [that is, unselfishly seek the best or higher good for others].' The whole Law and the [writings of the] Prophets depend on these two commandments.

Mathew 22:39-40 (AMP)

This is the first stone that must be used to slay the giants of anger and unforgiveness. Leviticus 19:18 (NIV) says, "Do not seek revenge or bear a grudge against anyone among your people, but love your neighbor as yourself. I am the Lord." What is great about this scripture is that it supports a lot of what was previously mentioned. Seeking revenge and bearing grudges stem from anger. He is telling us not to let those anger manifestations dictate how we act towards our fellow man; we should love them. Later in Mathew 22:37-38 (AMP) Jesus stated, "'You shall love the Lord your God with all your heart, and with all your soul, and with all your mind.' This is the first and greatest commandment." Basically, these three areas -heart, soul, and mind, are all that we are, and above all else, we must commit them all to loving God. There isn't an area left which can be occupied by anything else if those areas are full of love for God. Jesus went on to state that we must love our fellow man in the same way (Matthew 22:39-40 AMP). The power in these statements is how

He completed them, saying: "…all the law and the prophets hang on these two commandments." This speaks to the seriousness of the love we must have.

Why is this the first stone we must throw? It is because when we show love towards God and man in this manner, we are full of love and nothing else. Rather than being separate from Him in sin; we are in communion with Him and can act, think and live in the fullness of God. Love is the filter we must use before we respond and act towards our fellow man. You can't even pick up the other stones if you don't have love.

If you don't have love, then God is not in you, "Whoever does not love does not know God, because God is love" (1 John 4:8 NIV). 1 Corinthians 13:1-3 (NIV) references how without love, we are nothing and can gain nothing without it. In 1 John 4:12 (NIV), it describes how when love is in us, we experience the fullness of God, "No one has ever seen God; but if we love one another, God lives in us and his love is made complete in us." When God's love is made complete, then again, we have all His power to deal with and handle anything that comes our way. The three small words in 1 Corinthians 13:8 (NIV) "Love never fails" are truly experienced. Love can't fail against anger and unforgiveness because God is love. You have the victory, but only if you choose to do the commandment above.

When you love within your relationships, you are slaying the giant. You don't give Satan a crack to gain the foothold. You are not vulnerable to his deception to follow your flesh. You are full of love, and His love is complete in you. It's as simple as forgiving your spouse when they say or do something offensive. No retaliation, no plotting revenge or plans to get them back later. It is responding kindly to someone who is blatantly treating you wrong because that is what God does for us. For us to have all the unfailing power of God in us, there are several things we must do: 1) Believe that Christ is God's son, and then show others love. Chapter 13 of 1 Corinthians (NIV) says when we show love, God is in us. 2) If He lives in us, that means we have the same power Christ has. If we have the same power in us that Christ has, we have the same victory Christ has over sin and death because "…He has given us His spirit" (1 John 4:13 NIV). If love never fails, then it can't fail your marriage, various relationships or any other situation where you choose to act in love. Bottom line is, when I speak to my wife in a loving way, we have better discussions than when I am spiteful or mean-spirited. Without love, you will give in to where ever your anger takes you (which we know is not a good place). You will remember what the person did, create the list and take revenge. You will yell, cuss and do mean things because you are not rooted in love. You are separated from God.

Be encouraged by Ephesians 3:17-19 (NIV), "…And I pray that you, being rooted and established in love, may have power, together with all the Lord's holy people, to grasp how wide and long and high and deep is the love of Christ, and to know this love that surpasses knowledge - that you may be filled to the measure of all the fullness of God." When you are deeply rooted in love, you will have all of God in you, and you will preserve relationships versus destroy them. You will avoid the pitfalls of anger and unforgiveness. Ultimately, you will live the greatest commandments God wants us to perform, which is the foundation of all others. Love and forgiveness is what God did and does for us and using this stone means you will never fail and will have access to His power.

Stone 2

Above all, have fervent and unfailing love for one another, because love covers a multitude of sins [it overlooks unkindness and unselfishly seeks the best for others].

1 Peter 4:8 (AMP)

This second stone reinforces the mandate to love thy neighbor, but it ends with how love slays anger and unforgiveness. When you think about how Jesus died for the forgiveness of our sins, the correlation should be clear. The basis for love covering a multitude of sins is rooted in Jesus being able to cover our sins in the same manner. Remember, for God so loved the world, that He sent love to forgive us of our sins. When we choose to show love towards someone, it is our way of covering what someone else did to us; it is a choice. Just like God will throw our sins into the sea of forgetfulness - we can do the same when we love.

Everyone should use whatever gift you have received to serve others, "…as faithful stewards of God's grace in its various forms" (1 Peter 4:10 NIV). Until now, I have mostly referenced the more intimate relationships in our lives, but these passages begin to include anyone you may cross paths with. You should use what you have (i.e., your gifts) to show love towards them because He has given us diverse types of abilities. You can show love for others through your gifts, and it helps those around you to see the God in you and the many ways love can be expressed. It could be through your cooking, your time or repairing things for people - no matter what it is, you are going above and beyond the usual to help others. When you see the sins people commit against you and still show hospitality or use your gifts to help them, it does two things: 1) they see the various forms of love and 2) they will know God is in you because of the love you have towards them; even when it is undeserved. Rather than use your talents and gifts to destroy and break people or relationships, let love be the foundation to cover what they may have done and let love lead you.

Stone 3

Then Peter came to Him and asked, 'Lord, how many times will my brother sin against me and I forgive him and let it go? Up to seven times?' Jesus answered him, 'I say to you, not up to seven times, but seventy times seven.'

Matthew 18:21-22 (AMP)

Once you realize the importance and power of love, you need to understand the importance of forgiving in the eyes of God. Love makes you want to forgive and forgiving is an act of love. Not only did God show us forgiveness through His son, but He showed how much forgiveness He had to offer. Jesus's blood is shed for the remission of sins (past, present, future). That is how full and big His forgiveness is towards us. God just wants us to replicate in our way. God wants our level of forgiveness to be never-ending; just like His is as it was demonstrated through His Son.

When Jesus further explains the parable of the unmerciful servant to the disciples, it is not to give us a point when we can stop forgiving (Matthew 18:21-22). He is saying we should always forgive and keep doing it repeatedly.

Forgiving is not easy. The flesh is constantly trying to retaliate when it feels it has been wronged. I often go through a process to love and forgive in my marriage because it is just better than causing strife. I would be lying if I said it was easy. What I try to do is ask myself, "How is what I am about to say or do showing love? Will it build our relationship, improve this situation or escalate it?" When I do that, it helps me begin the process of forgiving and showing love. By no means does this mean you're a doormat. It just means, you are imitating God. I am trying to follow His example because I know it is best for my relationship or the situation. I don't want to allow unforgiveness to lead to grudges and other paybacks in our relationship. I have done that enough, and it doesn't help anything. Earlier we talked about not going to sleep angry. Ephesians 4:31-32 (MSG) says, "Make a clean break with all cutting, backbiting, profane talk. Be gentle with one another, sensitive. Forgive one another as quickly and thoroughly as God in Christ forgave you." In other words, don't wait. Be quick about it. Do it often. In the past, I made the mistake of being angry and not forgiving my spouse for days. This is not what God wants us to do. He wants us to thoroughly, quickly and continuously forgive; not partially, but totally forgive the person. In the past, I fell into the partial forgiveness trap. I forgave bits and pieces, but not all of what was on my mind. What happens? I have a list of offenses that gets longer and becomes the reason I get angrier over time. Forgive and move on. That is God's will, and it should be what we want to do for those around us.

Stone 4

Dear children, let us not love with words or speech but with actions and in truth.

1 John 3:18 (NIV)

This stone is all about putting your love where your actions are. You can't tell someone you love them and treat them horribly. Allowing anger to make you say and do all kinds of things to people is not love. There is a saying, "actions speak louder than words." The bible also says that faith without works is dead (James 2:26 AMP). There is a close relationship between saying and showing. This concept of acting implies that if you love someone, it should be seen in your actions towards them. Your actions are what give your words truth. You can slay the giant by what you say and by what you do. If you say I love you and I care about you, the truth will be in the showing. If you are angry and say and do things that are not right towards others - then when you say you love them, you are just talking.

I love my wife with all my heart. For years I would tell her I was thinking about doing special things for her. Unfortunately, I didn't do them or didn't do them consistently. The truth in my actions in her eyes was, "How special could I be if he doesn't follow through on what he says?" My feelings for her should have manifested through my actions. God is telling us not to be people who say we love, but be *doers* of love. Our love actions are so important to God that He challenges us to love our enemies. "But to you who are listening

I say: Love your enemies, do good to those who hate you, bless those who curse you, pray for those who mistreat you" (Luke 6:27-28 NIV). Again, this is a big challenge because Satan wants us to take revenge and to mistreat those who hate and mistreat us. Show love. Forgive over and over. Do it no matter how the person treats you. This is God's will.

Stone 5

Do not let unwholesome [foul, profane, worthless, vulgar] words ever come out of your mouth, but only such speech as is good for building up others, according to the need and the occasion, so that it will be a blessing to those who hear [you speak].

Ephesians 4:29 (AMP)

This verse describes how we should communicate towards each other. We all know the power of our words, but we are reminded in Proverbs 18:21 (AMP) that "Death and life are in the power of the tongue, and those who love it and indulge it will eat its fruit and bear the consequences of their words." When we choose love, we choose life. When we choose life, kind words come out of our mouths. God wants no words rooted in anger to come from us. Ephesians 4:31 (AMP) goes on to state: "Let all bitterness and wrath and anger and clamor [perpetual animosity, resentment, strife, fault-finding] and slander be put away from you, along with every kind of malice [all spitefulness, verbal abuse, malevolence]." All these things are the seeds to evil speaking. God is telling us we need to get rid of those things on the inside to prevent specific types of words coming out of us. He is saying, only those words which build others up, according to their needs, should come from us. This verse reiterates I John 3:18 (NIV), in speaking to God's will relative to our actions of love and our words of love. They are intertwined and an expectation of God's will for us to show love and forgiveness.

ENCOURAGEMENT FOR THE BATTLE

There are really two major ways God's actions helped me in my life with love and forgiveness. First, it was taking time to study anger. It wasn't something I did on my own, but I was asked to lead a bible study series. It was then when I began to understand what anger was, how Satan was using it against me in my life and what God really wanted us to do with the anger we naturally have. Anger was not intended for me to be mean and to say unspeakable things. It was placed in us to use it against sin and situations where people are being wronged. I was never to stay in anger, but to express it as God does. Shortly after the time I spent studying anger, I began to spend time studying love in Bible series, books and whatever I could get my hands on. My time reading about anger helped me see that anger and unforgiveness are defeated by love. Therefore, the more I understood and operated in love - the closer I got to God and the better I was able to fight anger and unforgiving episodes in my life. I am still on my journey. Out of the many topics in this book I was asked to discuss anger and unforgiveness. I believe it is God's way of helping me continue to learn and put into practice what I have digested.

The next best way to talk about God's actions is close to what I shared before with my wife. We have a lot in common, but our upbringing was different. Since she is more open with what bothers her, she has helped me be more open in the same way. I am very extroverted and have no problem expressing myself in any way - except when things occurred that I believed were an offense towards me. Our relationship has challenged me. I had to ask myself, what was more important - my love for my wife, or continuing to cause strife because of my anger? I don't believe in chance. God placed my wife specifically in my life. He knew that to help me get closer to Him in these areas, my spouse would assist me. Though she is the one who experienced my anger closet the most, it enabled me to be better overall with others when it comes to walking in love and forgiving. It helped me become a better person, father, husband, friend, and co-worker.

How God helps you understand love and forgiveness may be different for you. Perhaps this brief chapter is part of it. It is an area where I believe we must all fully commit. Too much of what He wants us to do and be in life are based on love. It starts with a commitment from the inside and should be seen by all. You can't talk, act or be holy and be absent of love. If that is you, you are missing the true God experience. Matthew 15:8 (NIV) says, "These people honor me with their lips, but their hearts are far from me." When you don't have love in your heart, you are absent from God. You also don't have the right filter to process your thoughts, words, and actions to prevent anger from leading you. We must actively apologize, actively forgive, speak kindly and show love. That is what God expects and what He wants us to do. Meditate on this: "Whatever you have learned or received or heard from me, or seen in me—put it into practice. And the God of peace will be with you" Philippians 4:9 (NIV). That is a pretty good trade-off. You do what God says and you gain God's peace. I'm all in - what about you?

There are many scriptures that detail what you must do to love in a Godly way and to forgive others. It starts with being born again; working on things that the flesh may tempt you to do is where the change begins. First, you must willingly choose the path most of the world does not want you to pick. Most of the world is angry and unforgiving. Reality TV is all about the fussing, fighting and unforgiveness of things people have committed. Matthew 7:13-14 (AMP) says, "Enter through the narrow gate. For wide is the gate and broad and easy to travel is the path that leads the way to destruction and eternal loss, and there are many who enter through it. But small is the gate and narrow and difficult to travel is the path that leads the way to [everlasting] life, and there are few who find it." Basically, when you choose to forgive and love people who have wronged you, it is the road less traveled - but stay the course. Renewing your mind is a key component to making better choices. Philippians 4:8 (AMP): "Finally, believers, whatever is true, whatever is honorable and worthy of respect, whatever is right and confirmed by God's word, whatever is pure and wholesome, whatever is lovely and brings peace, whatever is admirable and of good repute; if there is any excellence, if there is anything worthy of praise, think continually on these things [center your mind on them, and implant them in your heart]."

Getting your mind to think differently (renewing it) is important. When you fill it with things that are pure, it's hard to fill it with the vengeance, envy, malice, and bitterness caused by anger and unforgiveness. Romans 12:2 (NIV) reminds us, "Do not conform to the pattern of this world, but be transformed by the renewing of your mind. Then you will be able to test and approve what God's will is - his good, pleasing and perfect will." All of what has been stated are things you can use to renew your mind (and actions) to love and forgive separately from the world. Finally, true change starts within your heart. Proverbs 3:1-4 (AMP) says it best, "My son, do not forget my teaching, but let your heart keep my commandments; For length of days and years of life [worth living] And tranquility and prosperity [the wholeness of life's blessings] they will add to you. Do not let mercy and kindness and truth leave you [instead let these qualities define you]; Bind them [securely] around your neck, Write them on the tablet of your heart. So find favor and high esteem in the sight of God and man." This not only tells you what you should do; it tells you the benefits of love and forgiveness (and doing all that God commands us to do). Hopefully, doing what God wants just got easier.

> *It is a choice and it is our responsibility to act out of love and to forgive.*

What I have tried to stress thus far is the need to act. Be willing to make a change for the better. It is a choice, and it is our responsibility to act out of love and to forgive. It is God's will, and we should desire to please Him. We say we are Christians, which means we follow Christ. If that is true, then make the changes. Move on what you have learned and begin to see that the Lord is good. His Will, His Word are one in the same. We have discussed love and the reasons we should forgive. These two stones will greatly enhance the relationships you are in and those around you. You will be a different person. I would argue that you'll be a better person, of which both Christians and sinners alike will aspire to be like and be blessed by. You may never know the number of people who will benefit from what you say, show and do towards them and others through love and forgiveness. Where you go from here is up to you. Galatians 6:7-8 (MSG) says, "Don't be misled: No one makes a fool of God. What a person plants, he will harvest. The person who plants selfishness, ignoring the needs of others—ignoring God! —harvests a crop of weeds. All he'll have to show for his life is weeds! But the one who plants in response to God, letting God's Spirit do the growth work in him, harvests a crop of real life, eternal life." In other words, if you are angry and do not forgive, you will gain anger and all its corruptions. That is what Satan has for you. If you listen to the Lord your God (Spirit), you will receive eternal life. Not just salvation - but a full life full of the prosperity, peace, joy and a multitude of things God has for you. You know God's will - what will yours be going forward?

Consider Colossians 3:12-14 (NIV): "Therefore, as God's chosen people, holy and dearly loved, clothe yourselves with compassion, kindness, humility, gentleness and patience. Bear with each other and forgive one another if any of you has a grievance against someone. Forgive as the Lord forgave you. And over all these virtues put on love, which binds them all together in perfect unity."

I have written at length concerning the consequences of these giants and how allowing them to rule you has risks, consequences and is something fools do. Knowing God's will is really the act of going to the stream and pulling out the five smooth stones you can throw. You only need one to get the victory, but you must choose to throw it; if you don't, you may give Satan the foothold he so desperately desires. A good example is the story of Cain and Abel. We all know the story of these two brothers, but we may have overlooked the warning and description God gave to Cain, before he killed his brother. It says in Genesis 4:6-7 (NIV), "Then the Lord said to Cain, 'Why are you angry? Why is your face downcast? If you do what is right, will you not be accepted? But if you do not do what is right, sin is crouching at your door; it desires to have you, but you must rule over it.'" God knew that Cain's anger, driven by envy and jealousy, would lead to wrongdoing. As his anger grew, Satan crouched at the door waiting for the crack that anger causes. In this case, the transgression is the first physical murder. We must rule over the desire, and we don't have to do it alone. God wants us to slay these giants, and He has given us the stones to do it. Love and forgiveness is all you need.

MAKE IT PERSONAL

1. What people, things or situations do you find yourself repeatedly feeling angry about?

_____
_____
_____
_____

2. What specifically is it that angers you?

   _____
   _____
   _____
   _____
   _____

3. What benefit does being angry bring you?

   _____
   _____
   _____
   _____

4. What detriment or disadvantage does being angry bring you? Consider your attitude, behavior, and health.

   _____
   _____
   _____
   _____

5. If you have control over the thing that makes you angry, what can you do to change the situation to avoid developing these feelings?

   _____
   _____
   _____
   _____

6. If you do not have control, how can *you* change within the situation to avoid developing these feelings?

_____
_____
_____
_____
_____

7. Is there anyone in your life that you have not forgiven? Write their name below.

_____
_____
_____
_____
_____

8. Why have you not forgiven them?

_____
_____
_____
_____

9. What do you think will happen to them if you forgive them?

_____
_____
_____
_____

10. What do you think will happen to you if you forgive them?
   _____
   _____
   _____
   _____
   _____

11. Do you believe God's word? If yes, is it worth losing God's grace and mercy – His forgiveness of your sins, and ultimately His blessing on your life by not forgiving this person?
   _____
   _____
   _____
   _____
   _____

Forgiveness Challenge: Begin to pray for these people daily for 10 days. Do not pray about the situation. Do not pray that God takes vengeance on them. Pray that God blesses them and meets their needs. Pray a prayer that you would want someone to pray over your life. At the end of the 10 days, examine your heart to see if you are closer to being able to forgive them. Continue to pray for them until you can forgive them. Remember, you don't have to see them or speak to them to forgive them. They don't even have to know that they needed to be forgiven. Your act of forgiving others is totally about you and God, not you and that person. After the 10 days note how you are feeling below:

_____
_____
_____
_____

Love Challenge: Identify a situation or person that regularly angers you. Write three ways you can show love in that situation or to that person instead of responding in anger. The next time that situation arises, use one of these strategies to defeat your anger. Then reflect below how you felt about the situation.

1. _____
   _____
2. _____
   _____
3. _____
   _____

Reflection: _____
_____
_____
_____

Anger Challenge: Think about and write below what your typical response is when you are angry (e.g. yell, leave the situation, cry, hit, curse, silent treatment, etc.). Now think about ways that you can calmly and respectfully (even if you don't feel the other person deserves your respect) communicate how you are feeling. This does not mean having the discussion about your feelings but simply stating how you feel. Write down three or four simple statements below and practice saying them aloud. The next time you are feeling angry, use one of these statements to convey your feelings and add on the action you are going to take. For example: "That really upset me. I think we need to set aside some time to talk tonight." Or, "The last time this happened, I didn't say anything; but I have to let you know that this really bothers me, and I need for it to change if we are going to continue being friends." Write about how communicating your anger in this way made you feel.

Typical Anger Response: _____
_____
_____
_____
_____

Alternative Ways to Respond: _____
_____
_____
_____
_____

Reflection: _____
_____
_____
_____
_____

DAILY AFFIRMATION

I will use love and forgiveness to direct my relationship with those around me. I will love my neighbor with all my mind, soul and heart and use love as a filter for how I communicate and base my actions. Love will be the reason why I forgive over and over and over. I will not give in to my flesh and allow Satan to gain entrance. I will be strong in the Lord and in His love and will be able to show the fullness of love every day with the people with whom I come in contact. Praise God for His love towards me and the example of love and the forgiveness of sins through His son Jesus Christ.

Chapter Three

THE GIANT OF WORRY & FEAR

Barbara Everett

Hi! My name is Barbara, and I am a recovering worrier. I have been a worrier for about the last 10 or so years, but it had really gotten out of control within the last two or three years. And, when I say *out of control*, I mean living in an almost constant state of fear and anxiety while experiencing frequent chest pains and headaches throughout the day, and many months of waking up a couple of times a night in the middle of the night -if I even had the chance to sleep.

What did I worry about? It would probably be a shorter list if I told you what I didn't worry about. I worried about my husband, my children, my finances, my church, my job -pretty much everything! When the chest pains started coming a little more frequently, in addition to going to bed and waking up with a headache (which caused me to worry about suffering a stroke or dying from a heart attack), I knew I had to make some major changes in my life.

Now, before you ask, yes, I am a saved, born-again believer. I have been saved for over 35 years. However, knowing the Word and living the Word are two different things. When it came to worry, I never really applied the Word to that area of my life. I prayed about it all the time (well, it was me doing all the talking and hoping God was listening, but that is another story for another book), hoping God would do something about it. And He did. He sent little hints my way, reminding me to see what His Word had to say about it.

So, I did. By this time, it was my last resort, but it should have been my first and only resort. I have finally learned in times of stress and distress to remind myself of God's promises, who He says I am in His Word, and to pray for His guidance which will lead me to the end that I desire.

Our minds are designed with the ability and tendency towards meditation. However, we get to control what our minds focus on. I now choose to focus on the Word instead of the worry.

FIVE SMOOTH STONES

Stone 1

Do not be anxious about anything, but in every situation, by prayer and petition, with thanksgiving, present your requests to God. And the peace of God, which transcends all understanding, will guard your hearts and your minds in Christ Jesus. Finally, brothers and sisters, whatever is true, whatever is noble, whatever is right, whatever is pure, whatever is lovely, whatever is admirable—if anything is excellent or praiseworthy—think about such things.

Philippians 4:6-8 (NIV)

For most Christians, this is a popular verse and quoted a lot, but I want to dig deeper into what the verse really means. Why would God ask us not to worry about anything? First, excessive worrying not only impacts you mentally, but it also has physical side effects, such as headaches, high blood pressure, fatigue, rapid breathing, and heart attacks. And you already know that this is not how God wants His children to live. In John 10:10 (AMP), He tells us that the thief (aka Satan) comes to steal, kill and destroy, which is what worry does. It steals your joy, strength, and peace of mind. On the contrary, God sent Jesus the Christ so that we can "have and enjoy life, and have it in abundance [to the full, till it overflows]." Second, worry forces you to take your focus off God and place it on the situation at hand - the very situation that God allowed you to be in and the only one He can bring you out of.

Instead of worrying about anything, we are to pray about everything. By doing so, we can't help but stay constantly focused on God, because we are bringing every worry, concern, and issue to Him. While we are in prayer, we are not only to tell God what we need, but we are also to thank Him for what He has already done for us. When we do this, we are constantly reminding ourselves that if God did it before, He can most certainly do it again, and again, and again. I think you get the point!

Stone 2

But seek first his kingdom and his righteousness, and all these things will be given to you as well.

Matthew 6:33 (NIV)

Now, I strongly encourage you to start back at verse 25 to get a good understanding of what Jesus is trying to tell us. He starts off by telling us not to worry about food, drink, and clothes. It seems kind of odd that He says this because these things are necessary for living. But then He goes on to remind us that the birds eat every day even though they did not "sow, nor reap nor gather into barns" and the flowers grow into something beautiful to behold, but neither one did anything to make it happen. God took care of them. If He does this for birds and flowers, He will make sure we, His children, are taken care of. Why? Because a good father always meets his children's needs. Our job is to seek God's kingdom and His righteousness. So, once again, we are reminded to keep our focus on God and not to worry about anything else.

Stone 3

Humble yourselves, therefore, under God's mighty hand, that he may lift you up in due time. Cast all your anxiety on him because he cares for you.

1 Peter 5:6-7 (NIV)

You may be wondering how humbling yourself has anything to do with throwing your worries on God. Follow me here. When we begin to worry about a situation, this usually leads to us thinking of ways to handle it. This is prideful thinking. How? Because any time we begin to take matters into our own hands, we are essentially telling God that He can't handle it and we must do it ourselves. We are refusing to trust God, His plan and His solution to a situation that, many times, we got ourselves into. However, we are to put God above ourselves and situations (which is the meaning of humility) by casting everything we are worried about on Him because we know He cares about us and everything we are going through.

Stone 4

Cast your cares on the Lord and he will sustain you; he will never let the righteous be shaken.

Psalm 55:22 (NIV)

First, let me point out that *cast* means *to throw*. David is telling us not to just give our cares over to God, but throw them on Him! Whenever you throw something, you put a lot of force behind it because your intention is to make it go as far as possible. That is exactly what you are doing when you throw your cares on God. You are making them go as far away from you as possible. And when we do this, His Word says He will sustain, or take care, of us.

> Stone 5
>
> The Lord is my shepherd, I lack nothing. He makes me lie down in green pastures, he leads me beside quiet waters, he refreshes my soul. He guides me along the right paths for his name's sake. Even though I walk through the darkest valley, [a] I will fear no evil, for you are with me; your rod and your staff, they comfort me. You prepare a table before me in the presence of my enemies. You anoint my head with oil; my cup overflows. Surely your goodness and love will follow me all the days of my life, and I will dwell in the house of the Lord forever.
>
> Psalm 23 (NIV)

Whenever I begin to feel an anxiety attack coming on (which doesn't happen as often as it used to, praise God!) or I can't sleep at night, I say this Psalm aloud repeatedly until I can feel the anxiety going away or I drift back to sleep. David uses his work experience as a shepherd to explain how God, The Good Shepherd, takes care of us, His flock. Just as a shepherd makes sure the sheep are fed, safe and at peace, God does the same for us. I challenge you to read this the next time worry strikes. I guarantee that it will bring you peace in the middle of your storm.

ENCOURAGEMENT FOR THE BATTLE

It would be nice if situations that could cause us to worry didn't exist, but that's just not the case. Life will not be free from uncertainties, risk, or things and people that are out of our control. Control. Perhaps this is the thing, or the lack of it, that causes us to worry. We only worry about the things for which we do not know the outcome. We don't know the outcome because we are not in control of the outcome. If we were in control of the outcome, certainly the outcome would always be in our favor. We can, however, be assured that whatever may come, whatever situations may arise in our life that God is in control and He is always working things out for our good.

> *Worry will make you find a solution and to put plans in place that are not the plans God has for you.*

Our responsibility is to trust Him and to be led by the Holy Spirit in our actions, behavior, attitude, and decision-making. You see, worry can cause you to say and do things that you wouldn't normally say or do. Worry will make you find a solution and to put plans in place that are not the plans God has for you. Worry can have you entering relationships that you shouldn't be in and leaving relationships that you should stay in. It can have you leaving a job that God wants you to stay in or accepting a job that He does not want you to take. Worry can have a devastating effect on your life. Likewise, faith can have an enormously positive effect on your life. The wonderful thing about this is that we get to choose which one we are going to have.

Worry and fear are emotions brought on by the thoughts we have about our situations and circumstances. Guess who controls your thoughts? You are in total control of what you think about what is going on in your life. You can choose to think about the outcome you want or the worse-case scenario. You can choose to think about what is possible or what looks impossible. You can choose to think about success, or you can choose to think about failure. It's all a choice, and it's all your choice. Ultimately, you must make the choice daily to live in worry or to live in faith. I encourage you to choose faith. I encourage you to trust God, to trust His Word, and to trust the Holy Spirit that resides within you. Trust Him to give you direction. Trust in His ability to turn situations around. Trust that He can connect you with the people you need to know, take you to the places you need to go, and meet whatever need you may have. In Him is where all your solutions lie.

Matthew 6:33 tells us that if we seek God and his righteousness first, that is His way of being and doing, everything that we need, and desire will be given to us. And, Philippians 4:8 (AMP) says, "Finally, believers, whatever is true, whatever is honorable and worthy of respect, whatever is right and confirmed by God's word, whatever is pure and wholesome, whatever is lovely and brings peace, whatever is admirable and of good repute; if there is any excellence, if there is anything worthy of praise, think continually on these things [center your mind on them, and implant them in your heart." If we focus on living the way God wants us to live and keep our mind focused on things that are pure (God's word) and bring us peace, we can experience a worry-free life.

Does this mean that worry and fear will never come? Absolutely not; especially when we know that the enemy likes to attack our faith through fear. But, when it comes, don't let it take up residence in your mind. Begin to think about and speak out loud God's promises to you. Decide daily and in every situation to choose faith, to speak faith, and to trust God.

MAKE IT PERSONAL

When worry, fear, and anxiety come, use the following steps to take control of your thoughts. Once you get control of your thoughts, you can control your emotions, your behavior, actions, and attitude.

1. **Acknowledge It.** Don't try to cover up your fear with fake smiles and memorized scriptures of God's goodness. Identify what is at the root of the worry or fear. What is it that you are afraid of happening? What outcome are you worried about?

   _____
   _____
   _____

2. **Find Out What God's Word Says About It.** Identify scriptures that align with the outcome you desire. Write them down and keep them with you or commit them to memory. Accept God's word as the final authority on the issue. Decide to believe His word.

3. **Pray About It.** Once you've identified the specific thing you are concerned about, pray about it. Use the scriptures you identified in step two above to pray a specific prayer that calls on God to honor His word.

4. **Trust the Process.** Remember that your faith walk may take you along a different path than other people on the same journey. Some people will experience miraculous outcomes, while others have a longer and tougher road to their breakthrough. And, there are still many paths that could be taken between those two extremes. Whatever path you are on, trust the process that you are going through, learn what you can from the experience, and praise God

through the process. What are you specifically going to trust in this process?

_____
_____
_____
_____
_____

5. **Find Faithful Friends.** Identify two or three people that you can trust to keep your confidence, who are full of faith, and will come into agreement with you on what you are believing God for. They must be people who will pray for you, pray with you, and correct you when your words, actions, behaviors, attitudes, and decisions do not reflect faith. List these friends below.

_____
_____
_____
_____
_____

DAILY AFFIRMATION

I am not a worrier. I am a worshipper. I choose to relinquish control and follow the leading of the Holy Spirit. I choose to trust God over my feelings. I choose peace over anxiety, worry, and fear. God has already promised me victory. He has already committed to meeting my needs. He is my provider, my healer, my comforter, and friend. His grace and mercy cover me, and He works on my behalf to turn things for my good. I worship Him for who He is in my life, and I praise Him because of what He does in my life. I will no longer carry the burden of worry. I choose to worship instead.

Chapter Four

THE GIANT OF JEALOUSY & ENVY

Dr. Malaika M. Turner

I have dealt with jealousy and envy all my life. I can remember when comparing myself to others was common practice. Performing mental acrobatics was a daily occurrence, with thoughts such as:

"She's prettier than me."

"She has better clothes than I do."

"I wish my name was Nicole."

"I wish my eyes were gray."

"I'm too dark."

"I'm too hairy."

Everyone else was always better than me. Everyone else was always smarter. Everyone else's family was better than mine. Growing up, I can't remember a time when I was comfortable in my own skin. I always envied my friends - especially my white friends, and as a result, I continually looked for clothes, watches and any other item trending at the time. As a result, I envied everything and everyone. I always wanted what others had, and nothing satisfied that yearning.

I could always blame others for my issues with jealousy and envy. I could also believe the research which said not having a father tell me I was a beautiful little princess, contributed to my lack of self-confidence. Perhaps the dysfunction of my family situation contributed to my issues of envy and jealousy. Yes, I could blame others, and I probably have a legitimate right to blame others; but that would never produce anything positive and likely wouldn't result in a miraculous change in my life. In any case, for many years I envied others. Let's face it - to society, I was awkward; I wore braces, was hairy and had long feet for my height. I always felt uncomfortable, continuously peering at the *cute* girls, wishing I could be like them, look like them and have what they had. I was jealous. I wore jealousy like an extra small men's North Face coat. It fit snugly around me; it was warm, cozy and I was comfortable in it. Regrettably, I found myself repeating the same vicious cycle of befriending women who, in my mind, were more attractive than me, while simultaneously harboring jealousy for them. This resulted in me wanting more; more hair, lighter skin, more money to buy clothes to compete.

More, More, More! This is how greed makes its way into your heart. If you are jealous and envious of others, you want more. You continue to want more of what they have, while not being content with what you have been blessed to attain. You make the horrible mistake of praying that God changes what He so beautifully created. In your heart of hearts, you believe God made a mistake with you and it needs to be fixed. I remember being so angry with who God created. Why did I look like this? Why do I have these features? How could He name me Malaika - a name that in Swahili, means *angel*? How dare He? Why couldn't I grow up in a two-parent household with my biological parents? Why couldn't I have lighter skin and long hair? Why not, God? Why not! So, I lived my life jealous of everyone who had everything I wanted. I made friends with the very women I envied. I believed that if I established a close relationship with them, somehow would make up for what I didn't have in looks or material things.

In February 1993 came the answer to my issue of jealousy and envy. It was the beginning of my transition from jealousy and envy to a level of peace. This is when I accepted the Lord into my life.

FIVE SMOOTH STONES

Stone 1

For You formed my innermost parts; You knit me [together] in my mother's womb. I will give thanks and praise to You, for I am fearfully and wonderfully made; Wonderful are Your works, And my soul knows it very well.

Psalm 139:13-14 (AMP)

During my season of spiritual transition, this was one of the few scriptures that really took root inside of me. I remember attending a bible study in Philadelphia with friends, and this was one of the scriptures that impacted me and sparked a change. There was something reassuring about that scripture, yet something so unfamiliar. I wasn't accustomed to hearing that I was fearfully and wonderfully made; however, there was comfort in knowing that even in my mother's womb, God was creating, designing, developing and constructing me. Learning this as an adult was comforting. I am distinguished. I am set apart and special. Every detail of my being was intentional. Even with my hairy legs and long feet, I was - no, I am perfect for the purpose which God has called me to fulfill. Hallelujah!

Stone 2

But if you have bitter jealousy and selfish ambition in your hearts, do not be arrogant, and [as a result] be in defiance of the truth. For where jealousy and selfish ambition exist, there is disorder [unrest, rebellion] and every evil thing and morally degrading practice.

James 3:14, 16 (AMP)

While the passage in Psalm 139 challenged my feelings of insecurity, it didn't reach to the core of the jealousy issue. There was still one problem. Relying on the advice of several preachers I had heard, I looked for a scripture that would directly attack the heart of my issue – a word from God that was "...living and powerful and sharper than any two edge sword..." Hebrews 4:12 (NKJV). If I really wanted to see change, James 3:14 and 16 had to be in my arsenal. I had to recognize the chaos that jealousy could bring into my life. I had to remember what envy had caused me to do in the past. I didn't want to continue living that way. I didn't want these feelings of being less than (and they were just feelings, it was not truth) cause me to turn into someone I wasn't and didn't want to be.

Stone 3

Above all else, guard your heart, for everything you do flows from it.

Proverbs 4:23 (NIV)

It's very important to recognize that the heart is where the issues of life reside. If I am a person whose heart is full of jealousy and envy, my actions, my relationships and my attitude will be governed by those feelings. Even though I felt the way I did about myself and those around me, I knew that nothing good could from jealousy and envy ruling my life. It is important to understand that despite the mistakes I've made –that we've made –along the way, we are still wonderful in God's eyes. Many of us fail to believe this, but the scriptures tell us to:

Stone 4

> Trust in and rely confidently on the Lord with all your heart and do not rely on your own insight or understanding.
>
> Proverbs 3:5 (AMP)

We must trust that God loves us and has a purpose for our unique creation. We don't have to live in envy and jealousy. Yes, we may feel these emotions at times, but we don't have to allow them to take over our lives. Most of us don't intend to be jealous or envious. The feelings tend to sneak up on us. First, these emotions or issues start with being involved in an event or situation. Next, that event takes hold of the mind and our thought processes. We may see something or someone with our eyes and become desirous of them or what they have. Our mind becomes a cesspool of negative thoughts and visions that can turn our hearts into a sinful place. It may even start with being genuinely excited about a friend's accomplishments until thoughts begin to enter your mind about how their life compares to yours. Why is she getting married and not me? Why did he get the promotion and not me? Why did God bless her in her finances and not me? I pay my tithes too. So many things enter our minds, yet the thought - coupled with our own frustration or negativity, results in jealousy, envy or even greed. God's word provides us with instruction on how to overcome these giants.

Stone 5

> Finally, believers, whatever is true, whatever is honorable and worthy of respect, whatever is right and confirmed by God's word, whatever is pure and wholesome, whatever is lovely and brings peace, whatever is admirable and of good repute; if there is any excellence, if there is anything worthy of praise, think continually on these things [center your mind on them, and implant them in your heart].

Philippians 4:8 (AMP)

We must learn to change our mind's diet. Some of us should change what we take into our minds, which will help us become healthier in our walk with God. Galatians 5:19-21 (NIV) lists envy and jealousy as fruits of the flesh. As believers, we need to walk in the spirit and not in our flesh, which yields pain and hurt. We must make a conscious decision to control our minds and to rebuke the thoughts the enemy plants in our minds. When a jealous thought enters your mind, speak aloud against that thought by making a statement full of joy and kindness. When someone around you begins to speak words of jealousy or envy, speak up and change the conversation or leave the conversation. Do not give the enemy a place in your mind, because soon he will take over your heart.

God loves me. I know that now. God, has more than enough love for all of us, so know that He loves you, too. He also has enough blessings for all of us. Do you remember what Psalm 139:13-14 (AMP) says? God knows you intimately, having created you one stitch at a time, making you wonderful. He customized you, and He has customized blessings designed just for you. Be anxious for nothing. Believe God's word and follow His plan. That is where His blessing resides. There is no need to be jealous or envious because we're all God's favorite (Acts 10:34 NIV). You are His child and He desires to bless you.

ENCOURAGEMENT FOR THE BATTLE

It is God's will that we walk in the spirit and not in the flesh. Galatians 5:22 (AMP) says, "But the fruit of the Spirit [the result of His presence within us] is love [unselfish concern for others], joy, [inner] peace, patience [not the ability to wait, but how we act while waiting], kindness, goodness, faithfulness..." God desires that we walk in these seven fruits. Moreover, it is important that we recognize when jealousy and envy are creeping into our hearts. They may sneak up on us, but when they are recognized, it's important to make a conscious choice to walk in the spirit. So how is this done? God's will is for us to do what 1 John 1:9 (NIV) says, which is to confess our sins because God is faithful and ask Him to forgive us and cleanse us from unrighteousness. God is looking for brave souls who will admit they are envious, to admit they are jealous and be willing to submit to God's changing process.

As believers who are spirit-filled, there comes a time when we experience conviction. You know - that internal nudging or tightening in your gut that steers you in the right direction when you're headed in the wrong direction. Our will is always looking to fight against God's will. Galatians 5:17-18 (AMP) says, "For the [continually in conflict], so that you [as believers] do not [always] do whatever [good things] you want to do. But if you are guided and led by the Spirit, you are not subject to the Law."

The more we deny the flesh, the more we strengthen our spirit man and align our spirit man with the Holy Spirit which lives within us.

The more we deny the flesh, the more we strengthen our spirit man and align our spirit man with the Holy Spirit which lives within us. Jesus said in John 14:16-17 (AMP), "And I will ask the Father, and He will give you another Helper (Comforter, Advocate,

> sinful nature has its desire which is opposed to the Spirit, and the [desire of the] Spirit opposes the sinful nature; for these [two, the sinful nature and the Spirit] are in direct opposition to each other

Intercessor—Counselor, Strengthener, Standby), to be with you forever- the Spirit of Truth, whom the world cannot receive [and take to its heart] because it does not see Him or know Him, but you know Him because He (the Holy Spirit) remains with you continually and will be in you." This is one way we can obtain daily victory over the giants of jealousy and envy.

I realized that no matter how much I tried to rebuke jealousy or how many times I prayed that God would take it away from me, it had become so engrained in my nature, that to overcome it, I had to go to war with my thought-life. Every time a jealous or envious thought entered my mind, I would combat it by speaking affirming words, either about myself or the person or situation I was envious of. I reminded myself daily of how God had blessed me and began to be more appreciative of what He was doing in my life and less concerned about what He was doing in the lives of others. I also meditated on His word, which reinforced my faith in His promises to me. It wasn't long before I was able to rejoice when others rejoiced, and the power of jealousy and envy over my life was destroyed. I encourage you to try these steps for yourself.

MAKE IT PERSONAL

To help you get started, respond to the following:

1. Describe one awesome thing that God has done for you.

   _____
   _____
   _____
   _____
   _____

2. Write a sentence or two thanking God for what He did.

   _____
   _____
   _____
   _____
   _____

3. Describe one thing for which you are believing God now.
   _____
   _____
   _____
   _____

4. Find and write one scripture to attach your faith to that assures you of what God has for you.
   _____
   _____
   _____
   _____

5. Write down the names of three people you know that recently had something good happen to them and for whom, as a result, you were envious. Now, declare aloud a blessing on their lives. Finally, declare these words: *I am not jealous. Lord, you did not make a mistake with me. Father, give me peace of mind concerning who I am and what I possess.*
   _____
   _____
   _____
   _____

6. What are three things that you can do daily to prevent the feelings of jealousy and envy from entering your heart?
   _____
   _____
   _____

7. What are three things you can do when jealousy and envy are present in your heart to stop those feelings from overtaking you and impacting your attitude and behavior?

8. When you feel jealousy and envy lurking, it's helpful to have a believer available who will hold you accountable and pray for your change. James 5:16 (NIV) says, "Therefore confess your sins to each other and pray for each other so that you may be healed. The prayer of a righteous person is powerful and effective." Write down the name of someone who you can trust to hold this confidence, who will stand with you in prayer, and who will call you out when you are operating in jealousy and envy.

9. Write out your commitment statement below:

    I am committed to _____

_____

_____

DAILY AFFIRMATION

Today I trust in the Lord with all my heart, no matter how I feel in my flesh. I don't have to be jealous, envious or greedy because I'm fearfully and wonderfully made. God, you distinguished me, set me apart for your divine purpose. From this point forward, I will think on whatever things are lovely, pure and just and not concentrate on envying others or harboring jealousy in my heart. This giant will no longer take residence in my heart. I will walk in the spirit and not in the flesh and accept your love; the love you gave through your son who died on the cross for me.

Chapter Five

THE GIANT OF NEGATIVITY

Rev. Dr. Jacquita L. Wright-Henderson

I generally view myself as a positive person; but, when I took the time to focus on the words that I say and the thoughts that I think, I realized that I don't always think and speak life into situations. I had to check myself against the word of the Lord, which "discerns thoughts and attitude of the heart" (Hebrews 4:12 NIV). I found guidance on the impact of thinking or speaking negatively in Proverbs 18:21 (NIV), which tells us that "The tongue has the power of life and death, and those who love it will eat its fruit." This time of self-reflection helped me to realize that my thoughts and my words can bring life or death whether they are communicated through my thoughts or spoken aloud.

I noticed that when I was thinking negatively, I was looking at my situation in extremes such as good and bad or fair and unfair. A prime example is when I wasn't selected for the promotion that I wanted at work. In my disappointment, I immediately focused on how unfairly I was being treated. I convinced myself that my supervisors thought I wasn't doing a good job and that I would never be considered for other opportunities. I was overgeneralizing. Unfortunately, I was looking at this negative thought as being true in the present, and I even applied it to the future. It was hard for me to step back and look at my situation from a different point of view. I couldn't see how I was generalizing. Not only was I thinking negatively, but I also said some negative things that caused me to stagnate for a period because I spoke death into my situation and surrounded myself with others who did the same.

As I wallowed in my misery and negativity, I also engaged in some mental filtering. I focused on the negative aspects of the situation and disregarded the positive aspects. I was so busy looking at the fact that I didn't get the job I wanted, that I wasn't getting a raise, and all the negative aspects, that I couldn't see that I was blessed. I still had a job – a pretty good one, I had a flexible schedule; and I had peace of mind because no one was dropping new assignments on my desk or looking over my shoulder every five minutes.

Although I had a lot of things to be grateful for, it took me a long time to see that God was protecting me. God was watching over my comings and goings as the word tells us in Psalm 121:8 (NIV). God was protecting me from myself and guarding me from going into a situation that was not good for me. As time passed, I saw the expectations of the person who was given that position and I realized that it wasn't for me. I was watching Jeremiah 29:11 (NIV), "For I know the plans I have for you, declares the Lord, plans to prosper you and not to harm you, plans to give you hope and a future" come to fruition in my life. I prospered, found peace, and advanced to leadership roles in other areas of my life: the church, my family, and my sorority.

This was God's will for my life – to serve in the roles that he had for me. I had to follow Proverbs 3:5-6 (NIV) and "Trust in the Lord with all [my] heart and lean not to [my] own understanding." I needed to acknowledge Him in everything I did and allow Him to direct my paths. When I let go and let God rule my work situation, negativity receded, and positivity came forward.

Another situation, in which I find this scripture especially meaningful, happens every fall when new students arrive at the college. Part of my role as an administrator is to greet students and offer my assistance. Some students are excited and positive about a new beginning and the possibilities that lie ahead. Others seem totally opposite. However, when I talk to students, I find that they are open to being guided by others and their success is contingent on the words that they speak to themselves and the words that are spoken to them. It's important not to overgeneralize or look at these students as one extreme or another. Because of my revelation about thinking negatively, I encourage students to avoid dwelling on negative thoughts and to focus their minds on the positive.

This encouragement continues when I'm teaching my Student Success Course for new students. However, I often find myself working hard to remain positive when negativity creeps into the classroom. One student was especially challenging during a recent class. She responded to every statement that I made by shaking her head from side to side and emphatically stating, "I can't do that." After the third or fourth time that she responded in this manner, I asked her why she was in college. She responded, "In order to get a better job." I then began to share how she could reach her goal if she would try to do the things that she thought she couldn't. Then, I involved the entire class in helping to identify the steps that she needed to take to get started. I witnessed an immediate change in how she viewed her situation as we began to discuss her situation from the perspective of *I can* instead of I can't. Making the shift from negativity to positivity not only changed her perspective but it is likely to impact how successful she is in college.

> *Overcoming the giant of negativity is not about ignoring the bad things that happen in our lives or hiding our feelings about those things.*

I've come to learn that negativity - thinking negatively, speaking negatively, and having a negative perspective -can have a major impact on the quality of your life. How you think and how you speak will influence how you behave, the actions you take, and the decisions you make, which will inevitably impact your opportunities, your relationships, and your level of success. Overcoming the giant of negativity is not about ignoring the bad things that happen in our lives or hiding our feelings about those things. It's about intentionally focusing on what is good instead of that which is bad, acknowledging the possibilities and the potential rather than the impossibilities and what may be lacking, and seeing the beauty inside of an ugly situation. Our perspective influences our reality. A positive perspective will produce a positive reality, while a negative perspective will produce a negative reality. What we think and what we speak determines our perspective. Choose to think and speak the reality you want, not the one you see.

FIVE SMOOTH STONES

Stone 1

A good man brings good things out of the good stored up in his heart, and an evil man brings evil things out of the evil stored up in his heart. For the mouth speaks what the heart is full of.

Luke 6:45 (NIV)

The very best way to control what comes out of your mouth is to control what is in your heart. If negativity, pessimism, fear and perpetual dissatisfaction resides in your heart, inevitably that will be what comes out of your mouth. To change what comes out of your mouth requires a change of heart. You change your heart by changing what you allow to enter your mind through your eyes and ears. Consider what you listen to, what you watch, and what you read. Is it uplifting? Is it encouraging? Does it build your faith for the things of God or does it cause you to live in fear? Consider who you spend time with. Do they encourage you, motivate you or inspire you? Or, do they remind you of your limitations, your weaknesses, and your past? Do they see what can be or just what is today? You must make a conscious decision to surround yourself with good, positive and Godly people and things to ensure that your heart is full of good and God. Philippians 4:8 (NIV) says, "Finally, brothers and sisters, whatever is true, whatever is noble, whatever is right, whatever is pure, whatever is lovely, whatever is admirable -if anything is excellent or praiseworthy -think about such things." Doing this will cause your heart to be invaded with what is true, what is noble, what is right, what is pure, what is lovely, and what is admirable, and out of that heart is what your mouth shall speak.

Stone 2
The tongue has the power of life and death, and those who love it will eat its fruit.

Proverbs 18:21 (NIV)

Our words are powerful! The words we speak will bring good or evil, health or sickness, poverty or prosperity, life or death. It's like a king giving a command and his subjects hasten to do what he has said. When you speak a thing into the atmosphere, all heaven and hell hears your voice. The words you speak will determine which subjects begin to go to work to bring about what you've just spoken. If you speak negativity, brokenness, and death, hell begins to work to bring it to pass. If you speak positivity, wholeness, and life, heaven gets to work to bring it to pass. What you speak, you will live. Choose the power of life. Choose the power of good. Choose the power of wholeness. Choose to speak what you want in your life, not what you don't want. It's your choice. Choose wisely.

Stone 3
May these words of my mouth and this meditation of my heart be pleasing in your sight, Lord, my Rock and my Redeemer.

Psalm 19:14 (NIV)

As representatives of Christ in this world, we must seek daily to please God with our words and our heart. Focusing on speaking words that are meaningful and impactful, not only in our lives but in the lives of others, will please God. When faced with a situation that is bringing about negative thoughts and feelings, and you have plenty of negative things to say, hold onto your peace. Search your heart before responding to the situation. Seek to respond from a place of compassion, love, and forgiveness. Remember that the words you speak to others are either speaking life or death, and you have a responsibility to speak life into others just as you do to speak life to yourself. As much as it might satisfy your flesh to speak your mind, choose to speak from your heart, which reflects the heart of God.

Stone 4

And we know that in all things God works for the good of those who love him, who have been called according to his purpose.

Romans 8:28 (NIV)

It is the situations in our lives that cause us to think and speak negatively. But, if we can remember that in every situation, every problem that arises, everything that goes wrong in our lives, that God is working for our good simply because we love Him and are called according to His purpose, we can remain positive. There is no need to complain when God is at work in our situation. There is no need to fear when God fights our battles. There is no need to feel weak when God makes us strong. There is no need to lose sleep when God is our peace. There is no need when God is the provider of all things. If you believe this, speak it.

Stone 5

Rejoice always, pray continually, give thanks in all circumstances; for this is God's will for you in Christ Jesus.

I Thessalonians 5:16-18 (NIV)

It is God's will for you to rejoice, to pray and to give thanks in all circumstances. Why? Well, we just learned in Romans 8:28 that God is working everything for our good, so we may as well rejoice now because the outcome is sure. We can pray and give thanks at the beginning of a trial because we know that we will be victorious at the end of the trial. Maintaining a posture of prayer, praise, worship, and thanksgiving prevents us from focusing on what is wrong or bad. It keeps our hearts pure, our minds focused upwards towards God and not outwards towards the situation, and it keeps faith-filled words on our lips. When negativity wells up in you, pray and thank God. Don't let words leading to death depart from your lips.

ENCOURAGEMENT FOR THE BATTLE

Your thoughts are powerful! What you think will impact what you say, and it will impact what you do. Negative thoughts will come, but don't let them take residence in your mind. Take control of those thoughts! As soon as you realize the thought is there, choose to think differently. Reframe the thought into a positive one. If the negative thought continues to invade your mind, begin speaking the reframed positive thought aloud. You must train your mind to discard the negative and lock onto the positive. You can do it. The fact that you're reading this book means that you have a desire to

> *What you think will impact what you say, and it will impact what you do.*

take control of the things that have been controlling you, so you can experience victory in this life. Learning to control your thoughts is the first step.

Your words are powerful! Proverbs 16:24 (NIV) says, "Gracious words are a honeycomb, sweet to the soul and healing to the bones." You have the power to use your words to turn bitter situations and people into sweet, to bring about healing, and to alleviate discord. How much better is it to be known as the peacekeeper than the troublemaker, or the voice of reason than the voice of anarchy? When you have control of your thoughts, you can control your words. Being able to control your words gives you great power of influence. As a child of God, this influence is to be used to speak life, to bring peace, to edify, and to empower. You've got the power, now go and use it to change the world!

MAKE IT PERSONAL

Changing negative thoughts and words into positive thoughts and words requires the willingness to honestly assess our thoughts and words. Complete the steps below to start your journey:

Step 1: Select a bible verse to use as a guide for writing a prayer that will help you on your journey to thinking positive thoughts and using positive words. Consider starting a prayer journal to record your daily activities and prayer requests and then look back over time to see just how faithful God has been.

_____
_____
_____
_____
_____
_____

Step 2: List three negative thoughts that you've had this week:

1. _____

2. _____

3. _____

Step 3: Explain how you changed each negative thought into a positive thought:

1. _____

2. _____

3. _____

Step 4: List three negative statements that you spoke or heard this week:

1. _____

2. _____

3. _____

Step 5: Rewrite each statement to reflect a positive statement:

1. _____

2. _____
   _____
3. _____
   _____

PRAYER OF VICTORY

Heavenly Father, I thank you for this opportunity to learn more about your word and what it says about my thoughts and the words that I speak. Lord, I ask you to help me to change my thoughts and words so that they line up with your word. God, I ask you to show me how to judge myself, my thoughts, my words, and my actions according to your word. I ask you to help me not to judge others. Help me not to judge my brother or sister without cause and first looking at myself. Lord, please let me see the best in people and not try to find the worst in anyone. God, please forgive me of my sins that I've committed by thought, word, and deed against your divine majesty. Help me Lord to be who you've called me to be. Help me to improve myself first and then to be a help to others. God, I thank you for hearing my prayer. In the name of your son Jesus, I pray, Amen.

Chapter Six

THE GIANT OF GUILT

Stephanie L. Montgomery

In 1998, I lost my beloved mother suddenly, tragically and shortly after she turned 54. I went to college in the south, four states away from where we lived and when I graduated, I never returned home. Like most, I didn't truly appreciate my parents, their wisdom or guidance until I was on my own and far away from the comfort zone of my family. My mother then became my very best friend, my *Shero*. We spoke multiple times daily about everything and nothing. When the Lord called her home – to me, my family, the 4th graders she taught as an elementary school teacher, the cashiers at the grocery store and the many others whose lives she touched - she left way too soon and unfairly. Her passing distressed me to the point that, although I was never diagnosed, I'm sure I experienced what is best described as a nervous breakdown. Her death changed me. It angered me. Instead of the polite, quiet grace I inherited from my mom, I transitioned into a hardened woman who fiercely protected her son, her father and 14-year old sister. They were the only human beings who mattered in my life, and I made no apologies for the coldness I displayed towards anyone else.

 I was angry that my mother was taken from me so soon. How was I going to be a great mother to my own child without my mom correcting me or explaining how to do things the right way? How would I learn to cook certain meals the way she did? How was I going to help raise my fourteen-year-old sister who was fifteen years younger than me? I'd lived in another state since she was 4 and only saw her on holiday visits, so I was basically a stranger in her eyes. Who would calm me like only she could? Who would give me the sound advice only a mother can provide? Too many questions without answers. Anger consumed me.

In 2000, my father started dating and connected with a woman who was the opposite of my mother; she wasn't family-oriented, she wasn't outgoing, she wasn't friendly, nor could she cook. I despised everything about her, and because she wasn't a family-centered person, she wasn't interested in getting to know my sister or me at all. In short, the tension grew with my father in the middle of the chaos that already existed in my life. Although I knew I was raised better; to always show grace and kindness no matter what I received from others; I allowed my flesh to dominate my spirit.

Emotions escalated without restraint; and as it was evident this person had clearly captured my father's heart, the thought of her as a potential permanent fixture in our lives disgusted me. I was ugly. Mean. I purposed to intimidate her, isolate her and ignore her whenever the opportunity presented itself; and shamefully, I can admit to enjoying seeing her uneasiness. I was not saved during this time in my life, yet as I think back – I vividly recall on several occasions thinking: *God doesn't like ugly.* I wasn't raised in the church, but God's presence was always in our home and in my mother's words and actions. I knew better.

It was only God who kept me from completely going over the deep end after her passing; He continuously confirmed He was with me all the time, speaking to me always. It was God's voice lingering each time I intentionally was rude or nasty to my father's new love interest. I ignored the fact that my father deserved to find happiness again and to move on with his life. But I still felt guilt knowing my father was saddened at my behavior. I can be extremely stubborn, so despite the pangs of guilt concerning my actions, I continued displaying this behavior. While his new partner retaliated equally with rudeness, nastiness, and *tit for tat* actions; my negativity continued throughout the planning of my wedding and on my actual wedding day. As a result, my father and I had a huge blow up the morning of my wedding. Although I made it clear his girlfriend's attendance was not welcome, she came anyway, in blatant defiance. The fact that my father deliberately brought her despite my instruction had my blood boiling. My anger on that day is now memorialized in most of our wedding photos. I'm sure the photographer thoroughly enjoyed snapping photos of us yelling at each other during the father/daughter dance. I was positive he took those pictures on purpose, so the photographer was now on my list as well. I wanted to punch him in the throat.

The events of my wedding day caused the rift to spread like a disease. My mother's sisters were ready to attack my father's girlfriend, and my new husband was caught in the middle of wanting to support his bride while remaining respectful to his new father in law. All the while, feelings of guilt, regret and the sin I committed in failing to honor my father, continued keeping me up at night. All I had to do was apologize and stop being so mean, but another sin prevented me from ceasing my behavior – pride.

Not only did the feelings of guilt keep me from sleeping at night, they literally consumed me. My actions negatively affected all aspects of my familial relationships. It caused division. Those who felt loyal to my mother agreed with and supported my actions. Family members who acknowledged my father's need to move on lectured me about how disappointed they were in me, so now their names were also on the list of people I despised. It became too much. I wasn't properly honoring the wonderful spirit and legacy my mother left among those who knew her.

Finally, one year after my wedding, I knew the only way I could release the angst and poison which manifested inside me, was to do the right thing. I called my father's girlfriend and apologized. Literally, as soon as I said the words "I'm sorry for my actions," it felt like I lost 100 pounds of weight. I felt lighter and calm. I even smiled.

I learned through experience that guilt has a way of keeping you trapped in an emotional prison and burdened with the weight of what you've done wrong. Repenting -admitting the wrong and turning from the sinful behavior toward God and accepting God's forgiveness of your sin even if the person who you wronged does not forgive you, is the only way to release yourself from that prison and to drop the dead weight.

> *I learned through experience that guilt has a way of keeping you trapped in an emotional prison and burdened with the weight of what you've done wrong.*

FIVE SMOOTH STONES

Stone 1

The Lord is not slow in keeping his promise, as some understand slowness. Instead he is patient with you, not wanting anyone to perish, but everyone to come to repentance.

2 Peter 3:9 (NIV)

God is a loving father, standing ready to forgive you of your sins. He is patiently waiting for you to seek his forgiveness through your act of repentance. He does not want you to die in your sin or to die of your sin. There is no reason to feel condemned when God is standing with His arms outstretched waiting to forgive you, to love you and to show you who you are in Him.

Stone 2

Now may the God of peace Himself sanctify you through and through [that is, separate you from profane and vulgar things, make you pure and whole and undamaged—consecrated to Him—set apart for His purpose]; and may your spirit and soul and body be kept complete and [be found] blameless at the coming of our Lord Jesus Christ.

1 Thessalonians 5:23 (AMP)

Pure, whole and undamaged? Blameless? Is this possible? Indeed, it is, but only through the process of sanctification. Does sanctification mean that we will never do anything that will cause us to feel guilty? Absolutely not. What it means is that we are not forsaken. We can always return to the place of purpose that He has designed for us. Guilt moves us away from God, while our repentance brings us back to Him. Once we return to Him, we are blameless, and we are made whole and complete in Him through his love, grace, and mercy. God does not require us to be perfect. If He did, there would be no need for repentance or forgiveness. While He does not like or approve of our sin, He does not hold it against us.

Stone 3

So if the Son sets you free, you will be free indeed.

John 8:36 (NIV)

In the instant that you repent, God forgives you. Once He has forgiven you, you are free from condemnation, conviction, guilt, and shame. It doesn't matter what *they* say. It doesn't matter who else chooses to forgive you - or not. You are under no obligation to continue to apologize, to explain or to rehash what's in the past. When the Son sets you free your freedom is guaranteed and irrevocable. No one else has the power or authority to bind you in guilt when God has granted you liberty.

Stone 4
It is for freedom that Christ has set us free. Stand firm, then, and do not let yourselves be burdened again by a yoke of slavery.

Galatians 5:1 (NIV)

Guilt can be likened to a yoke. A yoke is bondage. Being in bondage is being restrained and oppressed, unable to move freely. Guilt will keep you from living the life that God designed for you to live. Guilt will cause you to refuse the blessings of God because you don't think you are worthy. The bondage of guilt will cause you to make choices that keep you on the path of unrighteousness because you believe that you are the sin rather than the sin being an act that you committed. Guilt has caused some people to take their life. This is not God's will for you. Stand firm in the liberty which God has granted you.

Stone 5
For if you forgive other people when they sin against you, your heavenly Father will also forgive you. But if you do not forgive others their sins, your Father will not forgive your sins.

Matthew 6:14-15 (NIV)

This scripture presents a very important key to remember. You cannot seek God's forgiveness if you are not willing to forgive others. For human-kind, the act of forgiveness has absolutely nothing to do with the act of seeking forgiveness. It doesn't matter if the person who wronged you apologizes. It is irrelevant that the person who has sinned against you has not sought out your forgiveness. It doesn't matter. You are responsible for releasing them from condemnation regardless of what they do. God is willing to forgive us far more than the seventy times seven He states in His Word and for things far worse than has ever been done to us. How can we go to Him asking for forgiveness and to be placed in right standing with Him, if we are not willing to show the same grace and mercy to others? Go before God with a pure heart, holding no ill-will against any man or woman. Then, you can receive God's forgiveness.

ENCOURAGEMENT FOR THE BATTLE

The world in which we live grows scarier daily and consistently reminds us that we are indeed living in the last of the last days. You will likely find yourself needing to forgive more often and perhaps needing forgiveness more often. Your faith will be tried. My prayer is that your faith and your Christ-likeness will always win over doing what is convenient, what benefits you, or what the world expects of you. Choose to do the righteous thing, but when you fail don't remain in that fallen state. Romans 12:2 tells us, "Do not conform to the pattern of this world, but be transformed by the renewing of your mind. Then you will be able to test and approve what God's will is - His good, pleasing and perfect will." Repent, while making sure that you are not holding any unforgiveness towards someone else in your heart, ask God to forgive you, accept His forgiveness, then saturate yourself in His word to renew your mind.

Renewing your mind is a daily process. The world is constantly bombarding you with sin, inviting you to participate and partake, trying to convince you that you are missing out on something, that doing what's right for you -what you want, is more important than doing what is righteous. The world would have you to believe that sin is just fun. But sin has deadly consequences. The process of

> *But when guilt comes, know that God has already provided the path to forgiveness and right-standing with Him.*

renewing your mind will help you to discern good from evil; fleshly desires from spiritual desires; God's voice from the voice of the world; and His good, pleasing and perfect will from the lust of the world. Renewing your mind will inevitably impact your thoughts and behavior, leading to fewer acts of sin and fewer bouts of guilt. But when guilt comes, know that God has already provided the path to forgiveness and right-standing with Him. Don't let a mistake or a wrong-doing keep you from God. Romans 8:37-39 (NIV) says, "No, in all these things we are more than conquerors through him who loved us. For I am convinced that neither death nor life, neither angels nor demons, neither the present nor the future, nor any powers, neither height nor depth, nor anything else in all creation, will be able to separate us from the love of God that is in Christ Jesus our Lord." Not even your sin can keep you separated from God unless you allow it to.

Don't let anyone convince you that God can't or won't forgive you, or that you don't deserve His forgiveness. God counted you worthy when He sent His son Jesus to die on the cross for your sins. He is waiting for you to accept His gift, to welcome you into His loving arms, and to celebrate your return home as the father of the prodigal son did in Luke 15:11-32. God loves you just as you are and through intimate fellowship with Him, you will become the person that He created you to be, in His image.

MAKE IT PERSONAL

1. **Identify the things you feel guilty about.** If you feel guilty about things you did to other people (even if they don't know it), include their names. Write these things down in simple "I" statements. For example, I lied on Mary and she lost her

job. Do not include any reasoning for your actions. Why you did what you did is not important. The fact that you are harboring guilt over it is.

_____
_____
_____
_____
_____

2. **Apologize.** If the person you wronged is aware of the wrong, apologize to them. Do not apologize for what you think you did wrong, apologize for what they think you did wrong. This could be done in person, over the phone, or by sending a hand-written letter. I caution you against sending an email, text message or using social media. Do not justify your actions or behavior. Simply apologize and ask for their forgiveness.

    If the person is not aware of the wrong, you'll have to decide for yourself if you want to make them aware and be prepared for the consequences of doing so. While apologizing will help to relieve your guilt, do not do it at the expense of ruining someone else's life or causing hurt that can otherwise be avoided. If apologizing is not the right thing to do, write the person a letter that you will never send. Read the letter out loud to yourself. Pray about the wrong you have done and ask God to repair what you broke, intervene in any confusion you may have caused and to bless the person for the pain you have caused them. Tear the letter up and throw it away.

3. **Ask God to forgive you.** Be specific about what you are seeking forgiveness for. Remember, he already knows what you did and the impact that you may not even be aware of, so no

need to try to hide details. After you've asked forgiveness, ask Him to help you to change your ways.

_____
_____
_____
_____

4. **Repent.** *Repent* means *to turn and go in the opposite direction towards God.* This means that you will change your behavior and you will not do these acts that have caused you guilt again.

5. **Forgive yourself.** Recognize that you are not your actions. Doing a bad thing does not make you a bad person. Look at yourself in a mirror and speak to yourself aloud. Tell yourself that you forgive yourself for whatever the actions were.

6. **Reflect.** Think about what you can learn from each situation, so you can avoid behaving in the same way again.

_____
_____
_____
_____

7. **Move on in liberty.** Do this for each situation you identify in step 1 until your conscience is clear. Focus on the future - doing better and being a better person. Focus on doing what pleases God and not what is easy to do or what satisfies your flesh. You've asked God to help you. When you seek Him out in challenging situations, He will guide you to the path of righteousness.

PRAYER OF VICTORY

Heavenly Father, I am so grateful that you are a loving and forgiving God. Thank you for showing me grace and mercy when I did not deserve it. Thank you for forgiving me over and over again; even when I did not forgive others. Your word says that if we confess our sins that you are faithful and just to cleanse us from unrighteousness (1 John 1:9). Lord, I confess my sins. Thank you for cleansing me. You also said that if I call on you when I am in trouble that you will answer me and deliver me (Psalm 50:15). I thank you that when I am in difficult situations, you are with me, that I hear your voice, and my soul is quick to obey. I ask that you heal those I have hurt and restore to those a hundred-fold anything that my words, actions or attitude has caused them to lose. I thank you for my liberty and the ability to move forward in life without guilt and shame. I love you, and I praise you. In Jesus' name. Amen.

Chapter Seven

THE GIANT OF PRIDE

Rev. Jack A. Claxton Jr.

Pride is defined, according to Dictionary.com, as a *high or inordinate opinion of one's own dignity, importance, merit, or superiority*. It is further explained that pride is an excessively positive view of one's own appearance, advantages, or achievements, and is often considered an offensive characteristic.

I discovered that pride is a destructive force. Pride can be an overvaluing of ourselves, esteeming ourselves to be wiser or better than we really are. I once had the attitude that "I've been there, I've done that, and I have that t-shirt!" When I was younger in the Lord, I thought I knew everything. I grew up in a certain church, and I thought I knew a lot about the Lord. I walked away from the Lord for a few years and then came back to the Lord. I thought I could pick right back up where I left off. I thought I knew a lot, only to find out I didn't know as much as I thought I did. That attitude kept me from receiving God's best during that time. I learned through this experience that pride can make you feel big and bad while you are letting it control you, but it can tear you down, destroy your family, and cause you to lose everything and everyone who matters to you. Eventually, pride will lead you to your lowest place, leaving you to humble yourself, seek forgiveness, and rebuild with the memory of all that was lost.

Pride also makes us vulnerable to many other sins. It's a major door-opener; it's a secret poison, a hidden plague, the engineer of deceit, the mother of hypocrisy, the parent of envy, the moth to holiness, the binder of hearts, the turner of medicines into maladies and remedies into diseases. It is the original and root of most of the notorious vices to be found among the children of men. It was pride that moved Herod to seek the blood of Christ. It was pride that put the Pharisees to persecuting Christ. It was pride that caused the wicked Queen Athaliah in 2 Kings 11:1 to destroy all the royal seed of the house of Judah that she might reign. It is pride that ushered in all the contentions that are found in the world. With pride comes nothing but strife.

As I've gotten older and closer to the Lord, I've learned that I don't really know much and that there's not much I can do in the absence of God's grace and favor. I decided not to let pride keep me from knowing God better and experiencing His best.

Throughout the Bible, we see that God has much to say about pride. For example, Proverbs 16:18 (NIV) tells us that "Pride goes before destruction and a haughty spirit before a fall." Obadiah 3 (AMP) states that pride and arrogance is deceptive. In 1 Peter 5:5 (NIV) we are told, "God opposes the proud but shows favor to the humble." Perhaps one of the most powerful scriptures is found in Proverbs 16:5 (NIV), "The LORD detests all the proud of heart. Be sure of this: They will not go unpunished."

> *When we take our eyes off God and focus on ourselves, we lose sight of the fact that He is who sustains us and equips us.*

Get rid of your pride before it drowns you in other sin. Leave that pride at the foot of the cross of Jesus Christ who voluntarily laid aside his glory. When pride takes the lead, it will lead you in the same direction every time -straight to destruction. A haughty spirit, one that doesn't want to listen to others, that thinks it knows everything and is never wrong will lead you to the edge of a cliff. When we take our eyes off God and focus on ourselves, we lose sight of the fact that He is who sustains us and equips us. It doesn't matter whether it's grief, a job, a business, or a relationship, we can't put our trust in ourselves. We can't be so good that nothing or no one else is good enough, or so smart that we can't listen to the wise counsel of others. Purpose to acknowledge the contributions of others to your success, be open-minded, willing to ask for help and to accept it when it is offered.

One of the first dangers of being prideful is developing the devil's character (being built up in pride) and his condemnation. A proud, unseasoned person has a condemnation like the devil. Look at Luke 10:18: "…I saw Satan fall as lightning from heaven." The devil's condemnation was that he must vacate heaven. The devil was given a very honorable position, but it wasn't big enough - it wasn't good enough for him. He wanted a bigger position; he wanted to occupy God's throne. He wanted to push God out of heaven, so he could expand and fill the throne room of heaven himself. God's response was to remove Satan from the position he had been given and cast him away from heaven. So indeed, the devil's condemnation is frightening; and so is ours if we fall into the pit of pride.

Paul says in 1 Timothy 3:6, "…being lifted up with pride he fall into the condemnation of the devil." If you don't want to be destroyed, stay humble, stay in the love walk and stay in the boundaries God has given you.

FIVE SMOOTH STONES

Stone 1

For by the grace given me I say to every one of you: Do not think of yourself more highly than you ought, but rather think of yourself with sober judgment, in accordance with the faith God has distributed to each of you.

Romans 12:3 (NIV)

You are great. When God created you, He created a masterpiece. But, without the Master, you are just another piece. See yourself as God sees you, but don't forget that all your goodness, all your skills, all your intelligence, all your beauty, and charm are attributable to the One who created you.

Stone 2
Recognize God's grace at work in our lives; with God all things are possible. When pride comes, then comes disgrace, but with humility comes wisdom.

Proverbs 11:2 (NIV)

This scripture states it so plainly; when we are prideful, we will eventually become disgraceful. However, when we operate in humility, we gain wisdom. Have you ever heard the saying, "Someone needs to take him down a peg or two?" It basically means that someone or something should cause an arrogant person's high opinion of themselves to be knocked down to a more realistic level. Proverbs 11:2 lets us know that we don't have to be knocked down or viewed as a disgrace if we keep our minds trained to recognize the power of God at work in our lives that enables and empowers us to do and to accomplish far above what we could on our own.

Stone 3
Pride brings a person low, but the lowly in spirit gain honor.

Proverbs 29:23 (NIV)

It's easy to become prideful, especially if you've experienced a lot of success, have a lot of material things, are smart, and people clamor to be in your presence. But, pride is a choice. We make decisions about who we are, our value to others (not to be confused with your worth), and how other people should view us and treat us. We make a choice to feed the hunger that comes with pride, surrounding ourselves with people who only reinforce what we think about ourselves. We can just as easily make the choice to be lowly in spirit -not seeking attention, applause, or praise for who we are or what we do; being more concerned about serving than being served and elevating others rather than seeking to be elevated. Would you rather have a lowly spirit and gain honor or be prideful and made low? The choice is yours.

Stone 4

Humility is the fear of the Lord; its wages are riches and honor and life.

Proverbs 22:4 (NIV)

Humility is a way of showing reverence to God. It takes the attention off you and places it rightfully where it belongs - on God. While it may seem to be an act of giving up something, perhaps notoriety, the love and admiration of people, or even the material things that come with having a fan base; humility brings the ultimate payoff. The Bible tells us that riches, honor, and life are the wages of humility. Choosing to walk in humility will advance you farther than choosing to walk in pride.

Stone 5

I can do all this through him who gives me strength.

Philippians 4:13 (NIV)

This scripture acknowledges that with Christ we can accomplish anything. Christ, the Anointed One and His anointing, bridges the gap in our skills, knowledge, and network. But this scripture says so much more. Not only *can we do* all things through

Him, but *we do* all things through Him. Whether we acknowledge Him or not, our successes are owed to Him. Whether we praise Him or not, our advancement is because of Him. Whether we give Him the honor that is due to Him or not, our victory is not of ourselves; it is because of Him. His grace and His anointing does not only show up when we call on Him. If we are His, He is in us, and He is strengthening us. He is equipping us and preparing us. We accomplish nothing without Him. We are nothing without Him. With Him, we can do anything, and without Him, our works are as filthy rags.

ENCOURAGEMENT FOR THE BATTLE

Defeating the giant of pride may be one of the toughest battles you fight. It not only requires you to change your opinion of God and other people, but you must also change your opinion of yourself. You must fight feelings of superiority and thoughts that belittle others. You must learn to be gracious and value the contributions of others. But if you are determined to kill this giant and win this battle, you can do it. Here are three things you can do to begin to shift your perception of self in light of the influence that God has in your life.

1. Repent. Ask God to forgive you for being prideful. God's forgiveness gives you a clean slate from which to start.

> If we [freely] admit that we have sinned and confess our sins, He is faithful and just [true to His own nature and promises], and will forgive our sins and cleanse us continually from all unrighteousness [our wrongdoing, everything not in conformity with His will and purpose].
>
> 1 John 1:9 (AMP)

2. Commit to changing by taking control of your thoughts utilizing the spiritual weapons that God gave you.

> The weapons of our warfare are not physical [weapons of flesh and blood]. Our weapons are divinely powerful for the destruction of fortresses. We are destroying sophisticated arguments and every exalted and proud thing that sets itself up against the [true] knowledge of God, and we are taking every thought and purpose captive to the obedience of Christ.
>
> 2 Corinthians 10:4-5 (AMP)

> Therefore, put on the complete armor of God, so that you will be able to [successfully] resist and stand your ground in the evil day [of danger], and having done everything [that the crisis demands], to stand firm [in your place, fully prepared, immovable, victorious]. So stand firm and hold your ground, having [a]tightened the wide band of truth (personal integrity, moral courage) around your waist and having put on the breastplate of righteousness (an upright heart), and having [b]strapped on your feet the gospel of peace in preparation [to face the enemy with firm-footed stability and the readiness produced by the good news]. Above all, lift up the [protective] [c]shield of faith with which you can extinguish all the flaming arrows of the evil one. And take the helmet of salvation, and the sword of the Spirit, which is the Word of God. With all prayer and petition pray [with specific requests] at all times [on every occasion and in every season] in

the Spirit, and with this in view, stay alert with all perseverance and petition [interceding in prayer] for all God's people.

Ephesians 6:13-18 (AMP)

3. Acknowledge the sustaining force that God is in your life.

   For the Spirit God gave us does not make us timid, but gives us power, love and self-discipline.

   2 Timothy 1:7 (NIV)

4. Recognize His creative power in designing you. Psalm 139:13-18 (AMP) describes the care and thought that God put into creating you:

   For You formed my innermost parts; You knit me [together] in my mother's womb. I will give thanks and praise to You, for I am fearfully and wonderfully made; Wonderful are Your works, And my soul knows it very well. My frame was not hidden from You, When I was being formed in secret, And intricately and skillfully formed [as if embroidered with many colors] in the depths of the earth. Your eyes have seen my unformed substance; And in Your book were all written The days that were appointed for me, When as yet there was not one of them [even taking shape]. How precious also are Your thoughts to me, O God! How vast is the sum of them! If I could count them, they would outnumber the sand. When I awake, I am still with You.

   Everything that you are and everything you can do is a result of how God created you.

5. Praise God for all that is good in your life.

> Every good thing given and every perfect gift is from above; it comes down from the Father of lights [the Creator and Sustainer of the heavens], in whom there is no variation [no rising or setting] or shadow [a]cast by His turning [for He is perfect and never changes].
>
> James 1:17 (AMP)

Remember what Matthew says in 23:12 (AMP), "Whoever exalts himself shall be humbled; and whoever humbles himself shall be raised to honor." Even if your heart has been full of pride, all is not lost. These verses tell us that we can change. We can humble ourselves; and in humbling ourselves, God will exalt us.

MAKE IT PERSONAL

1. List any areas where you recognize you need to walk in humility - such as family, friends, church, business or work relationships; accomplishments; material things; attitude.

   _____
   _____
   _____
   _____
   _____

2. Meditate on Psalm 139:13-18. Write below a thank you note to God for creating you as you are. Be sure to include everything that you take pride in, acknowledging that God is who deserves the credit.

   _____
   _____

_____

_____

_____

3. Each day for the next ten days, make it a point to compliment three people. They can be people you know or strangers. You can recognize something they said or did, how they look, or how they are dressed. Write how this made you feel.

_____

_____

_____

_____

4. When someone compliments you, instead of saying thank you, say Thank God or Praise God. Instead of accepting the credit, deflect it back to God. How did this feel?

_____

_____

_____

_____

5. Keep a gratitude journal thanking God for at least three things each day. Use this space until you get a journal. Your statements could be as simple as one word each.

_____

_____

_____

_____

PRAYER OF VICTORY

Lord help me to walk in love and humility and be attentive to my attitudes. Help me to be willing to listen to the voice of the Holy Spirit in this area of my life. Because I am walking in humility, I will not be deceived; I will not fall into the condemnation of the devil. God will not resist me, and I will be loved by God.

Chapter Eight

THE GIANT OF LOW SELF-ESTEEM

Carla Mitchell-Penny

"When you are put down enough in life, you start to believe what everyone says about you. When the people who are supposed to love you - like your parents, your family and your spouse, hurt and reject you; you find yourself withdrawing and finding comfort within the walls you formed to prevent others from getting in and inflicting the same kind of pain. Often, I found myself looking at a celebrity or a person who appeared to have it all together, wondering why God loved them so much more than me to give them what I so desperately wanted and needed."

As a thirty-six-year-old wife and mother of three, I would be lying if I said I never had any of the feelings that my friend shared with me. Maybe not to the same extent, but I have had my own struggles. I thought: if I could just lose those pesky ten pounds, I would feel much better about myself; if I got another degree, then I would be better than others, or if I obtained a certain level of wealth and prestige, then I would feel better about myself. If I can show the world that I have it all together, others will see how truly anointed I am, which would fill the emptiness inside. The operative word here, and the word I want you to focus on is had. I had my own self-esteem struggles; however, once I was able to get a firm understanding of my identity in Christ, I never struggled with that giant again.

Yes, I understand this is an awfully bold statement to make. I know what you are thinking: "You mean to tell me you never feel inadequate?

You never feel you are not pretty enough; not smart enough, not anointed enough or that you do not measure up to the standards of others? You never look at others who have more and wish you could be like them? Isn't it natural to feel like this sometimes?" The truth is, I used to have those feelings, but not anymore. So, does this mean that everything in my life is exactly the way I want? No. I still have weight to lose, books to read, money to save and an attitude to work on; but I know with Christ I can do and be anything. He has filled me up on the inside with overflowing confidence and my sincere prayer for you is that after reading this chapter you will feel the same way. Allow me to say I am by no means a professional or an expert on this topic, but I can share with you what thirty-six years of life experience has taught me and hope that you can be blessed as well.

* * *

Have you ever heard the saying "Those who live in glass houses should not throw stones?" What does it mean and how does this relate to low self-esteem? Well, in this book we are looking at the five smooth stones of scripture for fighting the Giants in our lives. But how do we throw stones at Giants when we are living in glass houses? To help you better understand; it all goes back to the conversation I had with my friend who said, "You withdraw and find comfort within the walls you put up to prevent others from getting in and inflicting the same kind of pain." How can we fight demons, Goliaths or any other giants when we are living in glass houses? The phrase *glass houses* refers to the images and appearances we place around our outer-selves, which often reflect and/or deflect positive or negative attention. It's that outer barrier we create to prevent people from seeing our own feelings of inadequacy. It's a façade; an image that's not real. We hide behind weaves, designer clothes, makeup, our education, our homes, our cars and our attitudes because we know that if someone were to get close to our heart, they would see what we are really hiding. Fear! When we are sold on the ideas of this world which say that image is everything; we begin to take the focus off what Christ says we are and begin to look at ourselves through the world's lenses. This is what I am referring to when I use the term glass houses.

> *We won't be moved by momentary strength, or moved by others - but like David, we will have a firm foundation of our strength based on purposeful, steady and consistent training.*

There are sporadic moments of strength when we feel ready to stand and fight against giants, yet we have not prepared for battle. When David was going to war with Goliath, he was fully prepared because of the hours he spent tending sheep. To fight against any giants in our life, we must spend time training ourselves for war. We must shatter the houses we currently live in; houses built by our past, by the words of others, by society and by our own expectations. We must change our thinking, our words and our actions for Christ to build our house - but this takes time and training (Luke 6:49; Psalm 127:1 NIV). Once prepared, we will not need our emotions to move us to fight the giants we face. We won't be moved by momentary strength, or moved by others - but like David, we will have a firm foundation of our strength based on purposeful, steady and consistent training.

FIVE SMOOTH STONES

Stone 1

Then God said, "Let us make mankind in our image, in our likeness, so that they may rule over the fish in the sea and the birds in the sky, over the livestock and all the wild animals, and over all the creatures that move along the ground. So God created mankind in his own image, in the image of God he created them; male and female

> he created them. God blessed them and said to them, "Be fruitful and increase in number; fill the earth and subdue it. Rule over the fish in the sea and the birds in the sky and over every living creature that moves on the ground.
>
> Genesis 1:26-28 (NIV)

And it was so. God made you special! God made you as an individual! God handcrafted you from the dust of the earth! God made you to rule, to be kings and priests, to have dominion over the things of this world. God loves each one of us so much. He sent His only son to be beaten, mistreated, abused and ridiculed so that we could be redeemed back to Him. God has placed gifts inside each of us, and we are born with purpose and destiny. We are blessed by God and considered to be His prime creation. The Lord of the entire universe has called you a son and daughter and an heir to His throne (Romans 18:15-17 NIV, Galatians 3:29 NIV)!

When it comes to fighting the Giant of low self-esteem, we must understand what God's will is for our life. The first stone of scripture I chose to use against this Giant, comes from the first book of the Bible; the book of Genesis. If you have been a student of the bible for any amount of time, you know that Genesis is considered a book of beginnings. Moses authored the book of Genesis and if you know his story - you know he was the man who led the children of Israel out of bondage and yet struggled with esteem issues. In Genesis 1:26-28 NIV, Moses reminds us just how important we are to God; He made us in His image to rule. So, in beginning your battle, understand that no matter what anyone may have told you; you are not a mistake or an accident - you were very much made on purpose with purpose!

Being a mother is perhaps one of the hardest jobs on the planet! I have three beautiful children. I am amazed every day at how completely different three children who all grew up in the same house can be. My oldest daughter is more introverted than the younger two; everything she touches or does seems to be perfect. She puts her heart and soul into her studies and is super brilliant; teachers compliment her work and are thrilled to have her in class. My second daughter is extremely independent and a true leader at heart. She can spend hours daily creating art and constructing all sorts of projects, she excels in athletics but must be pushed into her studies. My youngest, my son, is an extrovert and enjoys all the social aspects of school. He is a deep thinker, but a big partier; I cannot tell you how embarrassing it is doing the walk of shame to the teacher's classroom for a conference regarding how social my child is.

Although my husband and I love our children equally, each one requires a different parenting style. Yes, they are my children and created in my image, but they are independent of one another. Their uniqueness and independence bring a different flavor to our household. This is how we ought to be in Christ Jesus. Those of us who are in Christ share the same DNA; however, we were created uniquely and perfect in Christ!

Stone 2

For the LORD takes pleasure in His people; He will beautify the humble with salvation.

Psalm 149:4 (NKJV)

What an awesome piece of scripture for those who have received salvation. Here, David writes that God will beautify the humble with salvation. Wow! What great words for those who have questioned whether they are beautiful. I once saw a popular talk show and the guests were two young ladies who on the outside appeared very attractive - however, both talked about how on the inside they felt empty, unloved and hurt. Because of this, they were spending thousands of dollars and countless hours trying to improve their physical appearance.

I thought about those young ladies well after the closing credits scrolled up the screen. It took me right back to the whole idea of living in a glass house. The problem was not on the outside; no amount of physical adjustment would be enough to fix the problem. Please understand I am not against anything involving makeup, surgeries or other beauty habits one may have (I have often considered a little *nip and tuck*). It becomes an issue when that is how you identify yourself or when you portray an image and let others define who you are. Christ says that He will beautify the meek and humble with salvation, which means when you look in the mirror, the image reflected is not who you are. I am not the man in the mirror! I am a spirit. Christ beautifies my inner man. Once you accept Christ into your life, your inner man is reborn with a new image - His image. The salvation of the Lord shines from our inner man and is often visible through our outer man. Ok, yes, I know what you are thinking; "Well, my inner man is not the one trying to fit into those jeans," or "having a bad hair day" or "the one who was bullied because of my looks." This is true, but we cannot approach this giant from the outside in. We must approach this giant from the inside out! The more you allow Christ to beautify you on the inside, the more you will believe what He says about you! Try this little exercise: When you first wake up in the morning, look at your outer self in the mirror and examine every bump, wrinkle, and perceived imperfection; then begin to thank God for all that you see. Trust me, taking the focus off you and focusing on Him will bring everything into focus! This is the second step in shattering that glass house. It takes power away from the giant because you are facing your fears head-on. One thing I have learned about having self-esteem issues based on our physical appearances is that very little actually involves our looks or what we think. Most of our issues stem from what we think others will think about us. We must know that when Christ beautifies us, it is an eternal beauty that not only changes our inward appearance. It also delivers us from eternal damnation and saves us from a giant who is vying for our souls. This will ultimately have a significant impact on how we view ourselves physically.

Stone 3

Dear friends, let us love one another, for love comes from God. Everyone who loves has been born of God and knows God. Whoever does not love does not know God, because God is love.

1 John 4:7-8 (NIV)

I am confident I am loved by Christ and the love I find in Christ, can be extended to others. During the conversation with my friend (the one who I previously quoted in this chapter), she said; "When you are put down enough in life, you start to believe what others say about you, especially the people in your life who are supposed to love you like your family, your friends, and your spouse." This makes me wonder; how do I love when I don't feel loved or don't want to love? The answer takes me right back to the scripture referenced above - love comes from God. This is a fact you should bury deep inside your heart. People will hurt you, people will disappoint you, people will say they love you, but their actions may show otherwise. People will come into your life, then walk out. People will talk about you, then smile in your face. People will use you, people will abuse you, and people will break your heart. But God will love you always because God is love! This has a lot to do with self-esteem; it is difficult to have good self-esteem without love.

Love must be at the heart of all relationships we have - especially the one we have with ourselves. I've heard stories about young children from the same household who endured physical and emotional abuse from their parents. As they grew older, some displayed the same kinds of abuse towards others that they experienced. However, a few beat the statistical odds and led successful lives with loving families and spouses. When those children were asked what the difference was between them and the siblings they grew up with, the answer was always forgiveness and love.

When our parents disappoint us, when our spouses choose not to love us, and our friends turn their backs on us; we must let the love of Christ come in and flood our brokenness. We must extend the same love that Christ gives to us to others. I know from personal experience that it is hard to do. I have been hurt to my very core by family members, church members, and friends. At times, I even believed God must not have been with me to let me experience some of the hurt and pain I felt. But as I have grown in Christ and began ingesting the words written in the bible, I have found it easier and easier to extend and receive love. As I mentioned previously, having positive self-esteem has very little to do with your feelings and the thoughts you have about yourself, but it has a whole lot to do with who and what Christ says you are. Reliving or rehashing past wounds is equal to you standing in the middle of a field letting the giants in your life throw stones at you! God's word is the final law - the final authority. We can't rethink, or rehash old hurts; we must love and let go and believe that God loves us! This is a powerful stone which will defeat this giant every time.

Stone 4

I am convinced and confident of this very thing, that He who has begun a good work in you will [continue to] perfect and complete it until the day of Christ Jesus [the time of His return].

Philippians 1:6 (AMP)

God created you with a purpose! Comparing yourself to others is one of the fastest ways to develop low self-esteem. Wishing you were as smart, as pretty, as rich or had the talents of others will quickly lead you down a road of jealousy and envy - and once you travel down this road, it's hard to get back. We were each created in God's likeness, and He has given each of us our own purpose to fulfill. How can I find out what the purpose is for my life? This was a question posed to me from my oldest daughter. She said, "It seems like everyone else knows what they want to do and what they want to be, but I don't have a clue." She proceeded to say it was too late for her to pick up a sport or activity because she was too old. She was thirteen years old! So where does this idea come from? I have heard people three times her age question whether God really has a plan for their life. In my own life, I've had several different careers, goals, and aspirations - some of which had nothing at all to do with the other, but all were in pursuit of my purpose.

The ultimate answer to this question lies in what Christ says in the above-referenced scripture. We can be confident that Christ began a good work in each of us; meaning we don't have to envy what He is doing in anyone else. He created each of us uniquely. Even if we stop at the fifth word in this scripture, we can still build upon our self-esteem. If we only read *"I am convinced and confident…."* and didn't read further - we can defeat the giant of low self-esteem. Being confident in anything means that you believe in something with absolute certainty; there is no doubt. Having confidence comes from knowing who you are in Christ. Without Christ I am nothing! I learned this a long time ago. Every breath I take, every morning I wake up, everywhere I go, every relationship I have, and on my job - I need Christ. My confidence lies within Christ. I trust and believe He is going to complete a good work in me.

I mentioned previously that in my life I experienced various career paths, and in the process racked up thousands of dollars in student loans trying to figure out the work Christ is doing in me. I now know it is my call to be a teacher. Christ put that on the inside of me. The gift Christ has given me is to help build the kingdom of God. The same goes for you. What Christ has called you to do is to help build the kingdom of God. I got pregnant out of wedlock at nineteen years old. I remember bumping into a coach I had in high school at a local restaurant. She asked me how I could let this happen and said life was going to be really hard for me having a child early with no husband. She was right to a degree; life was hard being in college with a baby and without a husband, but what she didn't know was that I had Christ. With Christ as your support, the mistakes you made in your past do not matter. Put those things that are behind you, in the past; leave them there and keep moving forward. Be confident in knowing that from the moment you were born, Christ started a good work in you and He will complete it!

Stone 5

… that, regarding your previous way of life, you put off your old self [completely discard your former nature], which is being corrupted through deceitful desires, and be continually renewed in the spirit of your mind [having a fresh, untarnished mental and spiritual attitude], and put on the new self [the regenerated and renewed nature], created in God's image, [godlike] in the righteousness and holiness of the truth [living in a way that expresses to God your gratitude for your salvation]. Therefore, rejecting all falsehood [whether lying, defrauding, telling half-truths, spreading rumors, any such as these], speak truth each one with his neighbor, for we are all parts of one another [and we are all parts of the body of Christ].

Ephesians 4:22-25 (AMP)

This final scripture I have chosen to use for fighting the giant of low self-esteem opens with the ideas I have stated from the beginning of the chapter. This scripture tells you how to shatter those glass houses and get real with who you truly are; "put off the old self….and put on the new self." This is the first step in building yourself up in Christ. The walls you created to protect yourself from past hurts or from this giant, have taken you captive and must be taken down. Discard that old nature. There is sin in keeping an un-renewed mind and having a victim mentality. We will never learn to grow and mature if we are keeping ourselves comfortable in our own fears and our own ideas of who we are. The latter part of verse 22 states that these ideas are characterized by our previous lusts, which spring from delusion. The former man (our un-renewed self) would have us believe we are nothing and that what everyone said about us is true. But God says for us to grow in His righteousness, we must put aside this way of thinking - or as I like to say, "Shatter that glass house!" Verse 25 says we must reject all falseness. We are working towards holiness and right living. We must receive this into our hearts and confess this out of our mouths. We must know we are maturing in Christ and what we think we are lacking is not what Christ thinks of us!

ENCOURAGEMENT FOR THE BATTLE

So, what is God going to do to help me fight this giant of low self-esteem? Well, he's already done it! He created me in His image, and He sent His Son to die for all my sins. He made me beautiful when I accepted the gift of salvation. He loves me and teaches me how to love others. God will complete what He started in me. And, He is teaching me how to grow and mature in His righteousness. We must understand it is not the will of God for anyone who is in Him to feel, think or act in a way that is self-defeating. We are made beautiful, we were created and developed to be examples of Christ in this world, and we were made to be confident and find our confidence in Him.

> ***We must understand it is not the will of God for anyone who is in Him to feel, think or act in a way that is self-defeating.***

We must learn that each of us was born with a purpose and that through us God is able to complete what he started in us. We must believe that our righteousness or right living comes from Christ, not from our own works. You must understand that when Christ was crucified on the cross, you were forever weaved into the family of Christ. You became an heir and a possessor of all the gifts that He has for us in His word. Christ died for you so that you can have a right to live! He will defeat Satan and every demon that says otherwise! We have a role in understanding our own identity in Christ. We live in a society that focuses on images and how you look; however, we must understand that while man looks on the outside and judges, God looks at the heart (1 Samuel 16:7 NIV). Our minds must be renewed in His thinking. We have a responsibility to think of ourselves the same way Christ does. We cannot allow ourselves to be shaped and molded by this world. We cannot allow the words of others to dictate who we are. We cannot allow our environment to dictate who we are, and we cannot allow our family, friends, and peers dictate who we are either.

Our identity comes from Christ! It is time to wage war against every negative assault, which comes against us saying we do not measure up, we are not good enough, we are not qualified or loved; that we are not strong enough, wise enough or saved enough. We must boldly break out of these glass houses to destroy Satan's plan! My prayer for you is that you have the boldness to break out of your glass house, pick up a fist full of stones, take aim and defeat this giant with full force! Remember, with Christ, you will always win!

MAKE IT PERSONAL

1. What is your self-talk? What scripts play themselves repeatedly in your mind about your value and worth to your family, friends, employer, and the world at large?

   _____
   _____
   _____
   _____
   _____

2. Choose one script (one negative thing you typically say about yourself) and write it below. Then flip the script and write something positive about yourself that overwrites the negative script.

   _____
   _____
   _____
   _____
   _____

3. What is one negative thing that you say aloud to other people about yourself?

   _____
   _____
   _____
   _____
   _____

4. How can you change what you say to make a positive statement about yourself?

   _____
   _____

5. Knowing that you reap what you sow, how can you use your words to edify others in the same areas that you are challenged in?

_____
_____
_____
_____

6. In what areas of your life are you challenged with feelings of inadequacy?

_____
_____
_____
_____

7. What are three things you can do to make a change in this area?

_____
_____
_____
_____

8. Which one of the three things above will you commit to doing for the next 30 days to make a change in this area?

_____

_____
_____
_____
_____

9. Write out your commitment statement below:
   I am committed to _____
   _____
   _____
   _____
   _____
   _____.

10. Identify one person with whom you can share this commitment and who will encourage you and hold you accountable. Write the name below.
    _____
    _____
    _____
    _____
    _____

11. Identify at least three ways, whether through words or actions, this person can hold you accountable and encourage you.
    _____
    _____
    _____
    _____
    _____

12. Email, call or text this person immediately to let them know what you have committed to doing and how they can encourage you and hold you accountable.

_____
_____
_____
_____
_____

DAILY AFFIRMATION

I am a child of God; created in his image and developed by His love. Because God loves me, I know I am worthy of love –to give love and to receive love. Because God created me, I know I am beautiful and a reflection of God's heart. Because God is in me and works through me, I am confident that I am worthy, capable and deserving of God's best.

Chapter Nine

THE GIANT OF TEMPTATION & LUST

Dr. Melvin A. Jenkins

We live in a sexually-charged world. As such, inappropriate sexual activity is all around us. It seems like almost daily, we are bombarded with yet another sex scandal in the popular media. Whether it's a Hollywood celebrity, a professional athlete, or a politician, there seems to be no shortage of salacious details describing some sort of inappropriate sexual activity or behavior. In the world, there seem to be all kinds of perversions and voyeuristic desires. The internet and digital technology have allowed pornography and sexual temptation to flourish to the point where it can literally be viewed in the palm of one's hand.

Unfortunately, the church is not immune from sexual scandals and inappropriate activities. Time and again, we hear of large and small ministries, devastated because of sexual sin. Whether it's Catholic, Protestant, Evangelical, Mainline; the problem seems to spread across the spectrum like wildfire through dry brush indiscriminately. One thing for sure, however, is that this sin is pervasive and difficult to overcome. The problem manifests in many forms: adultery, fornication, perversion, pornography, and pedophilia to name a few.

Of course, sexual temptation and sin is certainly nothing new. The Bible is full of examples of men and women who were involved in inappropriate sexual activity. One needn't look any further than Genesis 9 (AMP) to find an example of a sexually-charged situation. The text refers to Ham's discovery of his father, Noah, in a drunken state and totally naked. There are several historical theories as to exactly what happened, including those which suggest some type of physical or homosexual activity. Although no one knows for sure, when one considers the outcome, it seems fair to suggest that something of an improper sexual nature occurred. Continuing through the Old Testament, the stories persist: Lot at Sodom and Daughters of Lot (Genesis 19 AMP), Judah and Tamar (Genesis 38 AMP), Gibeah (Judges 19 AMP), Sons of Eli (1 Samuel 2:22 AMP), David and Bathsheba (2 Samuel 11 AMP), Amnon and Tamar (2 Samuel 13:14 AMP), and Solomon (1 Kings 11:1 AMP). Moving into the New Testament, the issue of sexual misconduct appears again. The Lord Jesus dealt with promiscuity concerning the Samaritan Woman (John 4:17-18 MSG), and the woman *caught in the act* (John 8:4 AMP). Paul had a similar challenge in dealing with incest in the Corinthian church (1 Corinthians 5:1 AMP).

So, despite the power and presence of God, despite all the prayer and fasting, despite the commandments of God with their requisite threats of punishment, why does this problem seem to persist above so many others? And, how can we who have been given all things which pertain to life and godliness (2 Peter 1:3 AMP) overcome such a pervasive obstacle?

I'd like to suggest that for too long we have attempted to fight this battle using ineffective tactics. Let's consider how we typically treat an attack from the enemy. As an example, suppose we're provoked to anger by some circumstance and really wish to demonstrate that anger publicly. As good Christian soldiers, we generally use a combination of James 4:7, Matthew 4:10, and 2 Timothy 2:3 (AMP) to resist, stand and fight the wiles of our enemies. In this case, we would likely take a deep breath, gather our feelings and basically fight the urge to lash out angrily. Soon our tempers would cool down and we would continue with our routines, happy that we had the strength to overcome our emotions. That methodology generally works just fine in the case of anger (and many other emotional struggles for that matter).

However, sexual drive in humans is <u>not</u> an emotion as we see in 1 Corinthians 7:1-6 MSG:

> Now for the matters you wrote about: 'It is good for a man not to have sexual relations with a woman.' But since sexual immorality is occurring, each man should have sexual relations with his own wife, and each woman with her own husband. The husband should fulfill his marital duty to his wife, and likewise the wife to her husband. The wife does not have authority over her own body but yields it to her husband. In the same way, the husband does not have authority over his own body but yields it to his wife. Do not deprive each other except perhaps by mutual consent and for a time, so that you may devote yourselves to prayer. Then come together again so that Satan will not tempt you because of your lack of self-control. I say this as a concession, not as a command.

For most people, sexual urges are powerful and can be difficult to suppress. Like hunger or thirst, the urge for sex is a God-given drive which is a necessary part of the human experience. Our survival as a species depends on the fulfilling of sexual desires. Unfortunately, our flesh and/or the enemy continually attempt to pervert what God has created. Nonetheless, the significance of sex in our

> **Like hunger or thirst, the urge for sex is a God-given drive which is a necessary part of the human experience.**

lives cannot be diminished. Simply put, we as humans are hardwired for sex. Thus, to fight one's sex drive is to fight oneself.

The question remains, how does one overcome issues of sexual impurity? A close examination of scripture indicates that traditional methods simply won't work and were never intended to. We are in spiritual warfare, and the Bible often compares our battles with those of an actual military campaign. You see, when an army considers strategic (overall, long-term) objectives to defeat an enemy, multiple tactics must be employed to facilitate an effective victory. Tactical warfare involves specific maneuvers which must be undertaken based on the circumstances of the battle. When considering tactics, an army must know when to wage a frontal attack, when to advance from a flank, or when to retreat and regroup to fight another day.

And, so it is with spiritual warfare. The Bible says, "The weapons we fight with are not the weapons of the world. On the contrary, they have divine power to demolish strongholds" (2 Corinthians 10:4 NIV). We are in a battle. However, like an army, we must know which tactics to use, based on the enemies we face. In the case of sexual temptation, traditional stand and fight tactics will not, indeed cannot, work.

FIVE SMOOTH STONES

Stone 1
One day he went into the house to attend to his duties, and none of the household servants was inside. She caught him by his cloak and said, 'Come to bed with me!' But he left his cloak in her hand and ran out of the house.

Genesis 39:11-12 (NIV)

As humans, we have God-given sexual desires. When it comes to overcoming inappropriate sexual urges, it is important to know which tactic God commands that we use. The story of Joseph in Genesis 39 (NIV) provides an excellent example of how to effectively overcome a sexual temptation. According to scripture, an Egyptian officer by the name of Potiphar witnessed the work ethic of his slave Joseph and promoted Joseph to a most prominent position. This promotion was to the position of household overseer and enabled Joseph to work in the king's house on a regular basis. Joseph was responsible for running all aspects of Potiphar's house and as such, was in daily contact with Potiphar's wife.

Over the course of time, an attraction developed between them. With just a basic understanding of human nature, it's fair to assume that Potiphar's wife was as much of a temptation to Joseph as he was to her. As the wife of a prominent Egyptian officer, she likely was a well-kept woman with considerable assets to spend on herself and any potential paramour. As she and Joseph interacted daily, they likely conversed about professional and eventually personal matters. At some point, their interactions turned into a lustful attraction. The scripture indicates that over time this woman began to make ongoing sexual advances toward Joseph and though it seems unlikely that she had the physical strength to subdue him, if some drastic action wasn't taken, they would have likely *mutually* fallen into sexual sin. One day when her advances reached a point of maximum intensity - nearly too overwhelming to resist, Joseph decided to run from the situation, rather than submit to the temptation. He fled from her presence and out of her house.

Run from a spiritual attack? Somehow that just doesn't seem quite right for one of God's soldiers. Are we not instructed to put on the armor of God which enables us to stand firm against the enemy (Ephesians 6:10-18 NIV)? Of course, we are, but remember: different battles require different tactics. The notion of *stand*

and fight may work with some temptations, but with sexual challenges, there is only one proper course of action according to scripture: RUN.

Stone 2

Flee from sexual immorality. All other sins a person commits are outside the body, but whoever sins sexually, sins against their own body.

1 Corinthians 6:18 (NIV)

Flee sexual immorality. The Greek word that is translated *flee* here is *pheugo*. (Strong's Concordance) The literal translation of this word is, "to seek safety by flight, to be saved by flight, or to vanish." No part of that word suggests that we stand and fight. God's Word is clear that humans are not meant to overcome sexual temptation by standing and fighting. Recall that sexual urges are God-given for the survival of humanity. They are not meant to be directly fought or battled like other temptations. Rather, the tactic of retreat is instructed by God against these. Simply put, like Joseph, we are commanded to run when faced with a sexual temptation.

Stone 3

So I say, walk by the Spirit, and you will not gratify the desires of the flesh.

Galatians 5:16 (NIV)

Here the apostle Paul reminds his readers to move away from lustful situations. The word translated *walk* (*peripateo*) literally means *to make one's way or to progress* and is translated interchangeably *walk* or *go* throughout the New Testament (Strong's Concordance). The Biblical pattern continues: lust is something to be moved away from, not confronted head-on.

Stone 4

...and with your feet fitted with the readiness that comes from the gospel of peace.

Ephesians 6:15 (NIV)

We must utilize the Gospel through our feet sometimes. As stated earlier, our victory strategy, like that of any powerful army, employs various tactics based on the type of battle being waged. In this chapter, Paul speaks about the armor of God in waging war against the enemy of our souls. Notice, however, that Paul is intentional in mentioning the part of the armor that is to be used on the feet. Clearly, God intends for His children to use their feet sometimes in battle. It's up to us to know when the feet should stand, and when they should depart.

Stone 5

Flee the evil desires of youth and pursue righteousness, faith, love and peace, along with those who call on the Lord out of a pure heart.

2 Timothy 2:22 (NIV)

Once again, the word translated from flee is *pheugo*. Paul, in his wisdom and experience, admonishes young Timothy to run from the indulgences associated with youth.

ENCOURAGEMENT FOR THE BATTLE

"But thanks be to God! He gives us the victory through our Lord Jesus Christ" (1 Corinthians 15:57 NIV). "Yet in all these things we are more than conquerors and gain an overwhelming victory through Him who loved us [so much that He died for us]" (Romans 8:37 AMP). It is not His plan for us to continue in the bondage of sexual temptation. If it's true that we're more than conquerors, we should not be struggling with pornography for years. God wants His children free to enjoy the abundant life that His word promises us.

When it comes to sexual temptation, God instructs us to make tactical moves to overcome it. Lustful desires, because they are an outgrowth of our humanity, cannot be defeated by fighting or resisting. God's word clearly instructs us to flee or run from lustful situations. It seems to be a common misconception among individuals when tempted in a lustful situation that they can hold out or overcome by praying or standing strong. Despite their best efforts, they succumb to the temptation time and again. The lesson to be learned is that there is no shame or cowardice in running. In fact, running is specifically instructed by God to win this battle.

God's tactic against sexual sin is retreat.

The Word of God is clear that He forgives (1 John 1:9 NIV), but it is also clear that He wants us delivered from the bondage of sin (Romans 6:6 NIV). No child of God is meant to live in continual torment because of sexual sin. The key in this battle, as in all others, is to know the tactical plan to assure victory. God's tactic against sexual sin is retreat. Retreating in this situation is not a sign of weakness; rather, it's a sign of wisdom and strength! When faced with a lustful trial, get up and move away. This is God's plan for His children; this is God's purpose for us to achieve the victory He has promised!

In the case of Joseph, God brought a mighty deliverance. Granted, there was a period of trial and testing, but I believe that because of Joseph's wisdom amid a lustful situation, God later blessed him abundantly. I have known young unmarried couples who actively practiced fleeing from lustful encounters and were successful and blessed. On the other hand, I have seen many who tried to stand and fight and who lost miserably, primarily because sex drive (like hunger) is a part of human nature – and one cannot totally defeat one's own nature.

1 John 5:21 (AMP) tells us to "… guard yourselves from idols-[false teachings, moral compromises, and anything that would take God's place in your heart]." Temptation begins not only with what we see, but with what we hear, and with what we think about. When we listen to music that glorifies sexual exploits and conquests; watch movies, TV shows or music videos that show the sensuousness and sexuality of the human body, very real and nearly naked -if not totally naked - sex scenes; and look at sexy photographs on social media or in magazines; it is impossible to keep our minds from thinking about these things and imagining ourselves in these scenes. These thoughts and fantasies breed desire, desire breeds lust, and lust is a sure lure for temptation to show up in our lives. After giving so much time and attention to sex, we are morally compromised, not only is our flesh weak, but our spirit is weak as well, and we are so much more likely to give in to the temptation. Expecting to be able to *resist the devil and flee* from the physical temptation is unrealistic when we can't muster up the adrenaline to run from the visual and auditory temptation. Be careful about what you allow your eyes to observe and your ears to hear; opening your mind up to sexual immorality will eventually lead to the physical sin.

MAKE IT PERSONAL

Let's check what's entering your gates:

1. What music or artists do you listen to that deliver messages that are sexually explicit or seductive?

   _____

2. Which TV shows do you watch that regularly show sexual scenes or promote sexual immorality (pre-marital sex, infidelity, homosexuality, pedophilia, etc.)?

3. What magazines or online media do you read that regularly show sexually stimulating images?

4. Think about the amount of time you are watching, listening or reading any kind of media. About what percentage of that time do you think is spent viewing or listening to sexually oriented messages? What percentage of that time is focused on sexually oriented messages that promote abstinence, fidelity, faithfulness, and marriage?

5. What about these shows, media, images attract you?

6. How do you think constant exposure to these messages are impacting you?

7. What situations do you need to avoid so you can limit your exposure to sexual temptation?

8. If you were to find yourself in one of the situations you identified above, how would you negotiate your way out of the situation? What would be your way of escape?

9. Who are the people in your life who have already demonstrated that they are not willing to honor your commitment to avoiding sexual sin? What are you going to do about these relationships?

10. How can you successfully function as a man/woman of God amid such a perverse society?

Let's take this a step further by making a commitment.

What are you committed to changing to ensure that your fortitude in facing sexual temptation is strengthened? Write your commitment statement below.

I am committed to _____

PRAYER OF VICTORY

Father God, remind me when I am challenged by a lustful temptation that you have given me all things that pertain to life and Godliness. I realize that I live in a sexually-charged world, where I must be vigilant against human as well as digital temptations. Accordingly, I ask for your wisdom to know when to flee, and the grace to do so like Joseph. In Jesus' Name. Amen.

Chapter Ten

THE GIANT OF CONTROL & IMPATIENCE

Shawn Young Smith

A young man, in work attire, arrived at the station a little before his train was expected to come. He noticed other people standing on the platform waiting for the train. In his opinion, no one seemed to be as anxious as he was for the train to roll down the track. He paced back and forth on the platform, occasionally looking down the track, expecting the train to come any minute. He checked his watch, and he looked down the track again. For the next few minutes, the young man continued this pattern of checking his watch and looking down the track for the train. On a wall, in the station, he noticed a train schedule posted. He walked over to the schedule to check the arrival time of his train. According to the schedule, the train was definitely late. Finally, out of frustration, he found a transit worker to ask about the train schedule. The transit worker told the young man the train had been delayed and that it was out of their control. The young man looked at the worker in disbelief and wondered what he was going to do. The worker explained that sometimes trains are delayed for reasons beyond their control. And, with a calm voice, tried to comfort the young man by explaining to him the train will eventually come. This news did not make him feel any better. He walked away frustrated and very upset because he did not expect the train to be delayed. As the young man paced on the platform, the train he was waiting for pulled into the station and finally, he was on his way. As he boarded the train, he had a pep in his step because he knew he was finally moving closer to his destination.

A young lady dressed in a business suit entered the doctor's office, moving like a person on a mission. She approached the receptionist desk in a hurry and proceeded to inform the receptionist of her 1:00 pm appointment. The receptionist slowly looked up at the young lady and glanced at the clock, which read 12:55 pm. The receptionist let her know that she was a little early and must wait until her appointment time to be seen by the doctor. She asked the young lady to have a seat and said that someone will be with her shortly. The young lady looked at her watch, abruptly turned around and proceeded to take a seat in the waiting room. Before taking her seat, the young lady picked up a magazine to occupy her as she waited. She paged through the magazine but repeatedly looked up at the clock. 1:15pm. 1:20pm. 1:30pm. Now the young lady was fed up. She got up out of her seat, approached the counter and asked the receptionist, "When will it be my turn? I've been waiting and waiting. My appointment was for 1:00. It's now 1:30 and I am still waiting. What is the problem?" The receptionist calmly responded, "Ma'am, you must wait until your turn. The doctor will see you when your time comes. We know it's past your appointment, and we are moving as fast as we can to serve you, but some things are just out of our control." After 40 minutes had gone by, the receptionist asked the young lady to go to the back because the doctor was ready to see her. This news put a pleasant smile on the young lady's face.

These two situations are very different, but there are a few things that the young man from the train station and the young lady at the doctor's office had in common. Both had to wait for something that they needed. The young man needed the train to take him to his destination and the young lady needed to see the doctor for an annual checkup. The need was present, but the fulfillment was delayed.

Neither of them could change or control the reason why they had to wait. The young man could not control the circumstances leading up to the delayed train nor could the young lady change the reason why the doctor couldn't see her at her appointment time. The circumstances were out of their realm of responsibility. Both became frustrated when things didn't go their way, and they became impatient. Their attitudes did not display patience or self-control. They both lacked consideration for other people, especially the workers, who were neither to blame or able to fix the problem. They were rude and unkind to people who really had nothing to do with causing the delay. Finally, both of their needs were met at the appropriate time. Even though the young man's train was delayed, he was not denied the opportunity to get on the train and go to his destination. The young lady was seen long after her appointment, but she eventually got her opportunity to see the doctor. They were both delayed but not denied.

When the need to be in control is greater than trust in our sovereign God, impatience and frustration is inevitable.

The cause of frustration in both scenarios was the need to be in control of the situation. When the young man and the young lady lacked control of their situation, they became impatient and upset because it wasn't going the way they wanted it to go. They did not want to wait to see what was going to happen or trust the process; they wanted things to go as they had planned. When the need to be in control is greater than trust in our sovereign God, impatience and frustration is inevitable.

We live in a *give it to me now* society. If someone is not driving fast enough, we beep our horns in anger while quickly passing them and driving away speedily. We can't wait until we get to our destination to communicate with someone, so we text while driving. We go into debt because we can't wait and save for the things we want. We marry the wrong person because we can't wait for the right person to come into our lives. Why do we want everything now? Why is it hard for us to exercise patience while waiting for something we need or want? We need a change in our perspective. Instead of demanding everything now, we need to <u>N</u>ever <u>O</u>verlook <u>W</u>aiting.

We don't want to overlook the value of waiting. We don't want to overlook the lessons God teaches us through our waiting process. We don't want to overlook the preparation time waiting provides us. We want to maximize every moment in our lives, even in the waiting room.

FIVE SMOOTH STONES

Stone 1

I wait quietly before God, for my victory comes from him.

Psalm 62:1 (NLT)

According to Strong's Concordance, the Hebrew word for *wait* is *duwmiyah*, which means *stillness, abstractly quiet, and trust*. Waiting is synonymous with being silent and trusting in your quietness. Does this mean we sit in silence while we wait for God to move? No. Let's look at what it means to be silent while we wait. The New King James Version of the same scripture states, "Truly my soul silently waits for God; From Him comes my salvation." When we wait on God, it is our soul that waits. Our soul is made up of our mind, our will and our emotions. To conquer the giant of impatience, we must learn to keep our soul -our minds, will, and emotions silent.

We can do this by "bringing every thought into captivity to the obedience of Christ." (2 Corinthians 10:5b NKJV) We must be aware of what we are thinking and intentionally choose to think in a way that honors and edifies Christ, and that builds our faith. We must silence anxious and impatient thoughts and replace them with thoughts of victory and expectation of God's promises. Our mind is a battleground. We must fight against the thoughts that Satan implants in our heads. "Why is it taking God so long to move?" "Has God forgotten about me?" Thoughts like these will cause us to become anxious and worried about whether the promises of God will become a reality in our lives. When we choose to wait on God instead of coming up with our own plans and solutions, we are submitting and surrendering our will to the truth that God is in control and His timing is perfect.

When our behavior is controlled by our faith and not our emotions we are practicing waiting in silence. We may experience feelings of doubt, disappointment, and discouragement in our waiting season, but when these feelings come, we cannot allow them to control our attitude or impact our mental fortitude. We cannot become depressed or dysfunctional because things are not going as we planned. When our emotions are silent, we will behave in a way that pleases God. Psalm 101:2a (AMP) says, "I will behave wisely and follow the way of integrity."

The result of silently waiting on God is victory. Victory comes when we wait in expectation of God to fulfill His promise.

Stone 2

But those who wait for the Lord [who expect, look for, and hope in Him] Will gain new strength and renew their power; They will lift up their wings [and rise up close to God] like eagles [rising toward the sun]; They will run and not become weary, They will walk and not grow tired.

Isaiah 40:31 (AMP)

There are so many different meanings for the word *wait* in the Bible. In this passage, according to Strong's Concordance, the Hebrew word for *wait* is *qavah*, which means *to bind together, perhaps by twisting; to wait, look for, hope, expect; tarry, wait (for, on, upon)*. When we wait on the Lord and His timing, He will twist strength and hope around us. We receive strength to soar high like the eagle, to run the race marked out for us by God, and to walk by faith.

I remember hearing my pastor preach on flying with eagles. When the storm comes, the eagle uses the wind from the storm to lift it above the storm where it flies undisturbed. The eagle does not escape the storm, but it uses the storm to lift it higher. There's a lesson in there for us. As we wait on the Lord, we are like eagles who soar high when trouble comes. When the winds of doubt blow, we can use those winds to lift us up to higher place of revelation and truth, knowing God is in control and He has our best interest at heart.

Any person running a race knows that strength is needed during the toughest times, which is usually midway through the race. A runner needs strength to run and not give up when the race seems like it will never end. The Bible says, "Therefore, since we are surrounded by such a great cloud of witnesses, let us throw off everything that hinders and the sin that so easily entangles. And let us run with perseverance the race marked out for us" (Hebrews 12:1 NIV). As we run the race marked out for us and wait on the Lord to move on our behalf, we will gain strength to overcome weariness.

2 Corinthians 5:7 (AMP) says, "for we walk by faith, not by sight [living our lives in a manner consistent with our confident belief in God's promises]." In Hebrews 11:1 (KJV) we learn that faith is "the substance of things hoped for the evidence of things not seen." As we wait on the manifestation of things we are hoping for, we receive strength as we believe God for the evidence of what we do not see. Our faith walk causes us to believe God's plan is bigger and better than ours and allows us to wait patiently during the process.

Whether we soar, run or walk, God promises strength to us as we wait with expectation for God to move on our behalf. God is ready to give the strength we need to endure the process.

Stone 3

Wait for and confidently expect the Lord; Be strong and let your heart take courage; Yes, wait for and confidently expect the Lord.

Psalm 27:14 (AMP)

What does it mean to be strong and courageous? What is the difference between the two? *Amats* is the Hebrew word for *be strong*, and it means *to be alert in the mind, brave, bold, solid, and hard* (Strong's Concordance). In other words, to be strong, while you wait on the Lord, is to be alert mentally with firm and solid thinking. Being strong can mean physical toughness, but as believers, our minds must be strong, so we can "[successfully] stand up against all the schemes and the strategies and the deceits of the devil" (Ephesians 6:11 AMP). Paul encourages us in Ephesians 6:10 (NIV) to "be strong in the Lord and in his mighty power." The enemy tries to fool us into distrusting God through discouragement and disappointment. Discouragement comes when we believe God has forgotten us while we are waiting on the manifestation of His promise. Disappointment comes when we don't receive what we think we should have.

Chazaq is the Hebrew word for *be courageous*, which means *to strengthen, prevail, harden, become strong, be firm, grow firm, be resolute* (Strong's Concordance). In other words, to be courageous while waiting on the Lord is to conquer and prevail against any obstacle that could stand in the way of trusting God. It is doing what God says to do even we don't see the full picture. Courage, in the words of Napoleon Bonaparte, "isn't having the strength to go on – it is going on when you don't have strength." Courage is the fuel that keeps us waiting on the Lord with a good attitude. Courage gives us the power to prevail when we want to give up. Courage hardens us to difficulty, so we can hold on to the promises of God without wavering or giving up. Courage says, "I will wait on the Lord no matter how long it takes."

Stone 4

I waited patiently and expectantly for the Lord; And He inclined to me and heard my cry.

Psalm 40:1 (AMP)

According to the psalmist, we should wait patiently with expectation. The word *wait* in this passage is the same mentioned earlier in this chapter, *qavah* in Hebrew. It also means *to lie in wait for* (Strong's Concordance). When I read this, I immediately thought of the lion lying in wait to attack its prey. You see, the lion doesn't just run after the prey when it comes into its sight. It finds tall grass or a bush to hide in and gets into position waiting for the right time to overtake the prey. The lion lies in wait until it's time to make its move. Just like the lion, we may see our promise at a distance, but we must lie down low and wait. Getting down low is the position we must take; it is a position of prayer, of humility, and reverence to the plans and purposes of God. To be successful in obtaining the promise, we must lie down and wait patiently for the promises of God to manifest. God will give us guidance and direction on our next move.

The psalmist encourages us that as we lie in wait for the promise, God will incline to us and hear our cry. The Hebrew word for *incline* is *natah*, which means *to stretch out, extend, and offer; to bend and bow down*. The Hebrew word for *hear* is *shamu*, which means *to listen, give heed, to consent, agree, to grant request* (Strong's Concordance). So, our promise from God is that He will stretch out, bend and bow down to listen, give heed to and grant the request of the one who waits patiently for Him.

When we think of the notion of someone bending and bowing down, we can picture a child asking for something from their parents. The child may be speaking softly and the distance between their voice and the parent's ear is far away. The parent, to hear what their child is saying, will bend over and bow down to where the child is. The parent brings their ear close to the child's mouth, so they can hear their voice. The parent doesn't expect the child to come to them. The parent does the bending down to hear the voice of their child. God, in the same manner, will bend and bow down to listen to those who wait patiently for Him. When we pray, God bends down to hear us clearly.

What does God bend and bow down to listen to? God listens to the cry of His children. The Hebrew word in this passage for *cry* is *shav'ah*, which means *cry for help* (Strong's Concordance). The process of lying down in wait for the Lord and His promises is not easy. We need help from the Lord. We need His strength as we wait and seek His face. We need His power to fight off discouragement, fear, and worry. It's ok to cry out for help. When we, as God's children, cry out to our father for help, it is a praise to Him because we are confident that He will respond to our cry for help. Psalm 46:1 (AMP) says, "God is our refuge and strength [mighty and impenetrable], A very present and well-proved help in trouble." During our process of waiting, God is waiting to hear our cry, and He will bend and bow down to hear us and bring the promises to pass.

Stone 5

Hope in the Lord and keep his way. He will exalt you to inherit the land…

Psalm 37:34 (NIV)

Waiting with hope for the Lord. Again, we see the Hebrew word for *wait*, *qavah*. The definition that seems to fit best with this passage is *to bind together (perhaps by twisting) hence with a rope* (Strong's Concordance). As we wait, hope is like a rope that is tied around us. The main purpose of tying someone up with a rope is to prevent that person from putting up resistance and escaping, but it could also be to keep them still while giving them the help they need. There are some steps in the process of tying up someone. First, you must obtain the consent of the person or their guardian. Without consent, it's illegal. The Holy Spirit will not do anything that violates our free will. Second, at no time should the person be left alone while tied up. Jesus said, "…never will I leave you; never will I forsake you" Hebrews 13:5. Third, you should tie the rope around the person's hands. God doesn't want us to use our hands to try to fix and work on things he is handling. Lastly, the person should lie flat on the ground. Once again, this is the posture of submission. When the rope of hope is tied around us, we should be in a place of total surrender and submission. The rope of hope ties us up as we wait on the promises of God to fully manifest in our lives.

Following the Lord's path. According to Merriam-Webster, the word *follow* means *to go proceed or come after; to engage in as a calling or way of life; to be or act in accordance with*. Before we break down the definition for *follow*, let's look at what we are following. The path of the Lord is His course of life, mode of action and direction He has for us, which is found in His Word. We are encouraged by the psalmist to follow the direction the Lord has for our lives.

One of the definitions of *follow* is *to go, proceed, or come after*. Reading the Bible is good, but it is not enough. We must go and do what it says. According to another definition, we must engage in the Lord's course of life as a calling or way of life. Following the Lord's path is easy on Sunday morning at church. But the Lord's path for our lives should be an everyday goal. *To be or act in accordance with* is another definition of *follow*. We must evaluate ourselves daily on how our behavior and attitude align with God's ways and how we are directed in His Word.

Exalted and possess the land. The result of waiting with hope for the Lord and following His path is being honored by God to inherit land. The psalmist refers to land as territory, earth, ground, country, fields, and nations. God has promised that as we wait, tied up in hope, and follow the Lord's path, He will exalt or raise us up and give us the ground that rightfully belongs to us as children of God.

The last part of Psalm 34:37 (NIV) says, "…when the wicked are destroyed, you will see it." Not only will we take our rightful place as God raises us up in our workplace, families, communities and other areas of our lives, we will see the wicked given their just reward.

ENCOURAGEMENT FOR THE BATTLE

God's desire for us is to know and understand that He is in total control. The Bible says in Psalm 46:10 (AMP), "Be still and know (recognize, understand) that I am God. I will be exalted among the nations! I will be exalted in the earth." We must know that God is God. We must know that He is Sovereign, which means God is the ruler of the Universe and He has the authority, ability, and right to do whatever He wants. Not only should we know that God is in

> *Instead of being impatient, distraught and dismayed about the wait, we can take full advantage of that time by developing and preparing for His promise.*

control, we should recognize Him as the Sovereign God. The God who was not only there in the beginning, but who is the beginning. We also need to understand who God is -perceiving His intentions and His ways.

When we know God, we know that any time spent waiting is necessary. Instead of being impatient, distraught and dismayed about the wait, we can take full advantage of that time by developing and preparing for His promise. So, what can you do while in the waiting room?

Be transformed.

> Therefore I urge you, [b]brothers and sisters, by the mercies of God, to present your bodies [dedicating all of yourselves, set apart] as a living sacrifice, holy and well-pleasing to God, which is your rational (logical, intelligent) act of worship. And do not be conformed to this world [any longer with its superficial values and customs], but be [c]transformed and progressively changed [as you mature spiritually] by the renewing of your mind [focusing on godly values and ethical attitudes], so that you may prove [for yourselves] what the will of God is, that which is good and acceptable and perfect [in His plan and purpose for you].
>
> Romans 12:1-2 (AMP)

The mind is where the battle is fought. The powers of darkness want to take over our thoughts about God and His plan for our lives. Our minds must be transformed by renewing them with the truth of God's Word.

Develop patience.

> Consider it nothing but joy, my [a]brothers and sisters, whenever you fall into various trials. 3 Be assured that the testing of your faith [through experience] produces endurance [leading to spiritual

maturity, and inner peace]. And let endurance have its perfect result and do a thorough work, so that you may be perfect and completely developed [in your faith], lacking in nothing.

James 1:2-4 (AMP)

Patience has a chance to develop and grow in the waiting room. When we don't try to squirm out of our problems, then patience can develop into full bloom. Patience fully developed will cause us to be strong in character, complete and ready for anything, especially God's promises fulfilled.

Expect provision.

They all wait for You To give them their food in its appointed season.

Psalm 104:27 (AMP)

Maybe God is more concerned about the process rather than the promise. The promise is ours, but God wants us to be prepared for it. What good is it to have the promise and not be fully prepared for it? Allow God to provide everything you need while you wait.

Seize the moment.

In addition to all this, take up the shield of faith, with which you can extinguish all the flaming arrows of the evil one.

Ephesians 6:16 (NIV)

The waiting room experience is an opportunity of a lifetime. Leonard Ravenhill says, "The opportunity of a lifetime must be seized in the lifetime of the opportunity." The waiting room is a temporary holding place, and it won't last long. God has an expiration date on your wait, but while you are there, use the time wisely and with diligence. How do you do that?

1. **TRUST** in the Lord (Psalm 37:3a)
   Rely on and have confidence in Him.

2. **COMMIT** your way to the Lord (Psalm 37:5)
   Place your life in His hands.

3. **DO GOOD** (Psalm 37:3a)
   Make good choices. Do good to others. Let your life reflect the goodness of God.

4. **DWELL** in the land (Psalm 37:3b)
   Live your life. Do not hide or avoid other people. Be a light in this dark world.

5. **FEED** on God's faithfulness (Psalm 37:3b)
   Remember what God has done in the past - for you and for others. If He did it before, He can do it again. He is no respecter of persons, so what He did for someone else He can do for you.

6. **DELIGHT** yourself in the Lord (Psalm 37:4)
   Be joyful and be glad. Rejoice in what God has planned for you.

7. **REST** in the Lord (Psalm 37:7)

After you put your trust in the Lord, commit your way, do good, feed on God's faithfulness, and rejoice, you should rest in the Lord. Take a seat and relax, knowing that God's got it - whatever it is. The work is already done, the battle has already been won. You are just waiting for the manifestation in your life.

MAKE IT PERSONAL

1. What do you commit to doing to overcome the giant of impatience and develop a trusting attitude?

   _____
   _____
   _____
   _____
   _____

2. Complete the following sentences based on what you learned in this chapter. Use these sentences to make a daily declaration of your patience and trust in God.

   God's word says that I am _____.

   As I wait, my strength is renewed like the eagles. I gain new strength each day. I will Soar over _____. I will run through _____.

   I will walk by faith until _____. I decree and declare that I release the controls of my life into God's hands. I decree and declare that I will not become impatient as I wait for God's perfect will to be done. I decree and declare victory over discouragement and disappointment, worry and frustration. I decree and declare I will live a life full of joy because I know God is in total control.

PRAYER OF VICTORY

Heavenly Father, you are in total control, and I am not! You know what's best for my life and I do not. You see the big picture while I only see a small fraction. The plans you have for me are good. Help me to remember this truth when my heart wants to believe otherwise. Your word says be strong and courageous as I wait on the manifestation of your will in my life. Thank you for giving me the strength and courage to wait. As I wait, I know my victory comes from you. When I get tired of waiting, cause my strength to be renewed. Give me the ability to soar like an eagle, run without being weary and to walk without getting tired. Help me to choose to wait with hope for you to move and work on my behalf. I know when I cry out to you, you hear me. Thank you for hearing my prayer. As I wait on you, Lord, I will follow your path. I believe you will honor me and cause me to possess the land. In Jesus' name. Amen.

Learn More
About the Authors of
Five Smooth Stones:
Defeating the Giants Within

Dr. Cherita Weatherspoon

Cherita's mission is to engage, to elevate, and to empower. As a coach, author, and speaker, Cherita is dedicated to helping women release the guilt, become fearless, and step into their power and purpose as profitable entrepreneurs.

Cherita has worked with faith-based, education, non-profit, and for-profit organizations as a speaker, consultant, leader, and educator. As a Certified Professional Coach, Certified Job & Career Transition Coach, and author, Cherita knows how to use her words to connect with the audience and move them to action. As an Educational Specialist with a doctorate in Educational Leadership, she knows how to connect ideas and concepts that will equip the audience with the knowledge and skill they need to move forward.

She is the author of *Go! 10 Powerful Steps to Accomplishing Your Goals & Living the Life You Desire*; *Community College Leadership Defined: Identifying, Developing and Assessing the Competencies Necessary for Leadership Success in the 21st Century*; a contributing author in the International Best Seller, *My Big Idea Book*; *The Gratitude Book Project: Celebrating Moms & Motherhood*, and the *Black, Brilliant and Built for Success: Every Day Heroes and Heroines*. She is also the content editor and a senior contributor for Women of More Magazine.

Cherita is married to a wonderful and supportive husband and is a mother of four beautiful children. She is passionate about family, marriage, God, shoes, caramel, and being your personal power detonator.

Learn more about Cherita and her work at www.CheritaWeatherspoon.com and www.MissionCriticalConsulting.org. Find her on Facebook, Instagram, and Twitter at CoachCherita.

Virginia (Ginny) Herndon

"Your word, Lord, is eternal; it stands firm in the heavens." (Psalm 119:89 NIV). Knowing the Word and knowing the One Who is The Word are critical to walking the victorious life that we have been called to as children of God. It is a passion of Ginny's to mine the Word, to grow in the revelation of the love of this One Who is The Word, to take by faith what grace has provided and to share with others this pathway to zoe life.

For about ten years Ginny has hosted a Bible Study in her home, sharing His Truth and love to a group of women representing many different denominations, ages, walks of life and spiritual journeys. This weekly gathering is a water well for her and those who attend. It is one of many opportunities she seizes to speak about our identity as children of the Most High God and how confidence in that identity impacts our lives.

Ginny has had opportunities to teach the Word at her church's Healing School and seeks every opportunity to share God's love and God's Word because her appreciation for its power to produce life only increases. In addition, she serves as a member of the Timothy Team, the church's altar ministry, and as a mentor in the Wives in Training ministry.

Her educational background [Duke University, Psychology; Pennsylvania State University; Counseling] in counseling has been enriched by studying God's Word which holds the answers to all of life.

Prior to becoming a stay at home mother in 1981, Ginny worked as a counselor at the Burke Rehabilitation Center, White Plains, NY and then as a Trainer and Consultant at the Vocational Research Institute of the Jewish Vocational Services in Philadelphia, PA.

Ginny is an avid reader with much of the focus on knowing God, experiencing Him intimately and living in the blessing. Days are often filled by studying the Word, mentoring and encouraging others in their faith walk, and spending time with family and friends. She also enjoys cooking, baking, entertaining, gardening and traveling.

Ginny and her husband Randy have been married for almost forty years and are blessed to have three wonderful children, daughter in law, and three precious grandchildren.

Gregory Nicholson

Greg was born in Philadelphia, the youngest of 4 children. He grew up in a strong Christian, Pentecostal household. Although they were not what you might call "religious," church was at the center of everything they did. Greg was raised to seek God first and to live a Christ-like life. Greg saw in his parents a strong Christian and work ethic which provided examples that became the foundation of his beliefs, his concept of family, and work ambitions.

Greg describes his family as being very close. While they didn't have much financially, they found quality of life in their time spent as a family and love for one another. He learned later that prayer, tithing, and budgeting were how his parents managed to do everything they were able to do for their family. This was another foundational lesson that helped shape his life. When Greg left home to attend college at Howard University where he earned a degree in Finance and pledged Kappa Alpha Psi, he began to question his experience of God. He didn't stop believing, but he was more interested in *doing* life than in *not* doing life as he had been taught in his Pentecostal upbringing. Then he met Lisa Wilson who helped him look at God in a different way.

Lisa eventually became his wife, and they now have three children, Malik, Mycah, and Zaire. While they dated, they began attending church together. Once married, they relocated to Cincinnati OH where Greg met pastor Piphus, the man that taught him all of who God is and what is important to Him. Pastor Piphus helped Greg understand that being Christ-like is less about not doing certain things and more about living for Him. Greg learned that as you get closer to Him, He shows you more life and some things you just don't want to do anymore, they are less satisfying because of the life

God is showing you. Through Pastor Piphus, Greg began to pray, tithe and actively seeking God again. As he began to get closer to God, he found his purpose in his career.

Pastor Piphus and Deacon Meaux showed Greg that his gifts and talents were not just for the workplace but for the kingdom. He eventually taught his first class and eventually realized that teaching, mentoring, managing, building organizations, strategy, etc. were all part of His purpose for the kingdom. He eventually left Ohio and moved to Delaware, where he met Pastor Jerome at Seeds of Greatness. Pastor Jerome continued where Pastor Piphus left off and called on Greg to use what God had called him to do in the workplace in the House of God.

Greg is now one of the co-directors of the Seedlings Children's Ministry, a member of the planning and teaching team for the My Brother's Keeper Men's Ministry, and occasionally teaches Bible study and sessions in the Let's Make It Work Marriage Ministry with his wife. Greg acknowledges that his level of involvement in the church, his success as a mid-level manager in his company and having a close-knit family has all come full circle by God's plan.

Barbara Everett

Barbara Everett is an encouragement coach, writer, and blogger. She has a master's degree in School Counseling from Wilmington University and works as a Career & Technical Education teacher at her local high school. You can find her writing daily blog posts at www.BarbJEverett.com. On a more personal note, Barbara is a pastor's wife, mother of five, and loves to run, minister through liturgical dance and inspire women to create lives filled with joy, peace, and purpose. You can contact her at barb@barbjeverett.com.

Dr. Malaika M. Turner

Dr. Malaika Turner has worked in the student affairs division of Indiana University of Pennsylvania (IUP) for 18 years. She is currently the Director of Residential Living and Well-being, where she has had the opportunity to impact the lives of thousands of students and assist in the growth and development of student affairs professionals. Throughout her tenure at IUP, Dr. Turner has worked closely to assist at-risk students navigate the college system. Putting her passion into action, she co-developed and opened the Transition Success Office, designed to assist at-risk students during their transition from the IUP regional campus to the IUP Indiana campus. Her commitment to cultivating growth and confidence in at-risk students has also resulted in the creation of the S.T.E.P program, that was designed to help students STRIVE, TRANSITION, EMBRACE, and PROGRESS through college. Her dissertation, "Technology's Impact on the Learning Experience of At-Risk Digital Natives," is another example of her devotion to the improvement of at-risk students on college campuses.

Malaika manages a motivational brand, #ReviveToLive designed to motivate students, women, and other groups through numerous digital formats and print media. She has written numerous publications but is most proud of the first book she authored titled, *Walking In Step With God On Purpose*. Dr. Turner is currently working on a motivational ebook for students titled, From At-Risk to Ph.D. While her public speaking topics are custom designed for the institution/organization, her presentations never fail to mention a common message, and that is purpose. Dr. Turner champions the practice of goal setting, discovering purpose, and motivation. She has expanded her ability to motivate others, by using her gift of singing. In 2005, she was afforded the opportunity to sing the national anthem at a Pittsburgh Pirates game, before a crowd of 40,000 attendees. She stops at nothing when using her gifts and talents to motivate others.

Dr. Turner is a minister and praise and worship leader at Victory Christian Assembly where she and her husband, Pastor Theo Turner serve. She is the mother of two sons, Theo Malik and Tyree Marcel. She has an undeniable passion to see her sons succeed and discover their God-given purpose.

Rev. Dr. Jacquita L. Wright-Henderson

Dr. Jacquita L. Wright-Henderson is the Director of Planning and Institutional Effectiveness at Delaware Technical Community College where she oversees planning and assessment. In 2014, she was awarded a Presidential Certificate of Appreciation in recognition of her excellence and commitment to the College and the MSCHE Self-Study (accreditation) process. In addition to her various leadership roles in higher education, Dr. Jacquita has been an entrepreneur since 2000. Her business provides services that contribute to the success of local non-profit organizations and small businesses.

In the community, Dr. Wright-Henderson serves as the Pastor of Mt. Zion A.M.E. Church in Darby, PA. She is a life member of Alpha Kappa Alpha Sorority, Incorporated where she serves as secretary of the Newark, DE chapter and member of the International Leadership Development Committee. Dr. Jacquita is also a member of the Delaware ACE Women's Network, A.M.E. Women in Ministry, and enjoys life as a contributing author, keynote speaker, life coach, wife, mother, and grandmother.

Stephanie L. Montgomery

Stephanie is a diversely-creative writer and profound communicator with exemplary editing skills. Both of her parents were educators, and it is through her mother's teachings, she adopted a love of writing through poetry. She believes she is following the plan God has for her life by utilizing the gifts and talents He has blessed her with.

With over 17 years of leadership and managerial experience, Stephanie has an established and proven track record in administrative oversight, performance management, staff development and utilization of effective communicatory mediums for diverse audiences. She is grateful for the experiences and lessons learned throughout her professional career and development; however, her true passion for writing never ceased. As a well-regarded talent within the local writing industry, Stephanie possesses outstanding and endearing interpersonal skills and fully believes anything in this life is attainable and possible when you have a positive spirit and put your trust in God.

Her professional background includes 17 years of operational leadership and management; however opportunities through her church allowed her to engage in her passion through writing plays and spoken- word pieces for various events since 2007. These blessings and opportunities – and faith in God, enabled Stephanie to start her own consulting business in 2012, Unique Communications Concepts. Through her business, Stephanie performs a variety of writing services including; Speech and Creative Writing, Editing and Proof-Reading, Grant and Proposal Writing, Web Content and Voice-Over Services (non union). In addition to managing her consulting business, Stephanie is the Creative Editor for Chosen

Butterfly Christian Publishing company and is currently a Program Manager and Adjunct English Instructor at Delaware Technical Community College in Wilmington, Delaware.

She holds a Bachelor of Arts degree in English from North Carolina Central University and is also a certified Grant & Proposal Writer. Stephanie loves to laugh and has a great sense of humor. She is a compassionate woman who loves the Lord, with a down-to-earth and peaceful spirit.

Rev. Jack A. Claxton, Jr.

Jack was born in 1947 in the small town of Salem, NJ. Growing up in such a small town, Jack learned early on that family and community were important. He spent his time as a youth in the Assembly of God church and was active with other youth in Royal Rangers. His high school sweetheart Cindy grew up in the same town and, upon graduation, they were married. Jack spent those early years after graduation in the New Jersey National Guard and getting an early start in customer service and sales with Sears and Roebuck Company. He and Cindy had one child, a daughter, and lived a fairly typical suburban life throughout the 70s and early 80s. Jack spent a great deal of time in various sales positions while his wife was a stay at home mom.

In the early 80's, Jack was the owner of a local general store and deli that primarily serviced the men and women of the local power plant. His wife played a vital role in helping him run the business and they were very successful together. In their spare time, they were active boaters, spent a great deal of time at the Jersey shore, and Jack was an avid golfer.

God steered them in a different direction in 1985 when the General Store closed, and they began attending Victory Christian Fellowship. In 1988, Jack graduated from Victory Bible School and from 1989-1992, pastored his own church, Chesapeake Praise Ministries. From 1989-1993, he took courses from the Rev. June Austin and in 2000 he graduated from Chesapeake Bible College and Seminary with a bachelor's degree.

Since that time, Jack has spent a great deal of those years as a salesman for Elmer Door Company, working the lower Jersey shore area. He is an Elder at Seeds of Greatness Bible Church. He often speaks at special events and teaches in their Healing School. After the passing of his wife in 2009, he spends his free time enjoying his Harley Davidson and connecting with his daughter and grandchildren whenever he can.

Carla Mitchell-Penny

Carla J. Mitchell-Penny has spent many years facilitating and teaching various Bible classes and Christian study groups. Carla believes wholeheartedly that there is "No weapon or circumstance that the enemy can throw at you that Christ will not give you the power to withstand!"

Professionally, Carla is a Human Resources Labor Relations Specialist and has a master's degree in Human Resources from Wilmington University in Delaware. Carla is originally from Fairmont, West Virginia and considers herself a true coal miner's daughter and country girl at heart. She currently lives in Delaware with her wonderful husband Brian and three amazingly brilliant kids.

Dr. Melvin A. Jenkins

Bishop Melvin A. Jenkins, Ed.D. was born and raised in suburban Philadelphia, PA and from an early age took a strong interest in the church and gospel music. Before he completed high school, Dr. Jenkins was an active musician and was involved with several local gospel groups.

During his pursuit of a B.A. degree in Liberal Arts at Penn State, Dr. Jenkins received the Call to Ministry. He was later ordained and eventually promoted to Assistant Pastor of Unity Church of Jesus Christ in State College, PA. Some years later, the Lord moved the Jenkins family to Indiana University of Pennsylvania (IUP) where he earned a master's degree. It was there they founded the IUP Voices of Joy gospel choir in 1988 and Victory Christian Assembly in 1990. Dr. Jenkins earned a doctorate in Developmental Education from Grambling State University in 2002 and is currently a full professor and department chair at IUP.

Victory Christian Assembly has grown steadily since its inception. In addition to the "home" church in Indiana, PA, the Lord has birthed two additional ministries from Victory: New Beginnings Christian Fellowship in Punxsutawney, PA and Impact Fellowship on the campus of Penn State Harrisburg, PA. In recognition of the grace and calling on his life, Dr. Jenkins was promoted to the office of Bishop in 2013, under Fountain of Life International Fellowship led by Dr. Gerald Loyd. Bishop Jenkins feels inspired to start several more college-based ministries over the next few years, as the Lord has given him tremendous grace in this area of church planting.

Shawn Young Smith

Shawn Cherise Smith was born in Philadelphia, PA to John and Brenda Young. At an early age, Shawn received the Lord and decided to live for him. Shawn attended the Philadelphia Church of God, under the spiritual covering of Bishop Michael A. Clayton. Under his teaching and through the direction of the Holy Spirit, Shawn made a lifelong commitment to know God and to make Him known.

Shawn is a woman of God, with a word from God for the people of God. Shawn has a passion for seeing God's people grow in grace and in the knowledge of Him. Because of this passion, God has opened many doors for Shawn to speak at revivals, seminars, prayer breakfasts, workshops, etc. Shawn also has a desire to see all God's people worship him in spirit and in truth. She has led and sung on praise and worship teams within the Body of Christ. Her life verse is Psalm 34:1, *"I will bless the Lord at all times and his praise shall continually be in my mouth."*

Shawn works as a high school educator and strongly believes in educating and preparing our young men and women to be as successful as they can be.

Currently, Shawn is a faithful member of Seeds of Greatness Bible Church, where Pastor Jerome Lewis is the pastor. Shawn is active in various ministries within the church. She serves on the ministerial team, dances with the Word in Motion Dance Ministry and teaches in the Seedlings Children's Ministry. Shawn is also the servant-leader of W.I.S.D.O.M. ministries, a weekly women's conference call focused on studying the women of the Bible.

Shawn is the proud mother of two "kings-in-the-making," Vincent and Jonathan Smith. Shawn is a dedicated mother, faithful friend, loving daughter, and sister, but most of all, she is a servant of the Most High God.

you the power to withstand!" Professionally, Carla is a Human Resources Labor Relations Specialist and has a master's degree in Human Resources from Wilmington University in Delaware. Carla is originally from Fairmont, West Virginia and considers herself a true coal miner's daughter and country girl at heart. She currently lives in Delaware with her wonderful husband Brian and three amazingly brilliant kids.

Dr. Melvin A. Jenkins

Bishop Melvin A. Jenkins, Ed.D. was born and raised in suburban Philadelphia, PA and from an early age took a strong interest in the church and gospel music. Before he completed high school, Dr. Jenkins was an active musician and was involved with several local gospel groups.

During his pursuit of a B.A. degree in Liberal Arts at Penn State, Dr. Jenkins received the Call to Ministry. He was later ordained and eventually promoted to Assistant Pastor of Unity Church of Jesus Christ in State College, PA. Some years later, the Lord moved the Jenkins family to Indiana University of Pennsylvania (IUP) where he earned a master's degree. It was there they founded the IUP Voices of Joy gospel choir in 1988 and Victory Christian Assembly in 1990. Dr. Jenkins earned a doctorate in Developmental Education from Grambling State University in 2002 and is currently a full professor and department chair at IUP.

Victory Christian Assembly has grown steadily since its inception. In addition to the "home" church in Indiana, PA, the Lord has birthed two additional ministries from Victory: New Beginnings Christian Fellowship in Punxsutawney, PA and Impact Fellowship on the campus of Penn State Harrisburg, PA. In recognition of the

www.ingramcontent.com/pod-product-compliance
Lightning Source LLC
Chambersburg PA
CBHW030437010526
44118CB00011B/671